1

The Blind African Slave,
or Memoirs of Boyrereau Brinch,
Nick-named Jeffrey Brace.

Containing an Account of the Kingdom of BowWoo, in the Interior of Africa; with the Climate and Natural Productions, Laws, and Customs Peculiar to That Place. With an Account of His Captivity, Sufferings, Sales, Travels, Emancipation, Conversion to the Christian Religion, Knowledge of the Scriptures, &c. Interspersed with Strictures on Slavery, Speculative Observations on the Qualities of Human Nature, with Quotation from Scripture

By

Benjamin F. Prentiss
[1774-1817]

THE
Blind African Slave,
OR MEMOIRS OF
BOYREREAU BRINCH,
NICK-NAMED
JEFFREY BRACE.

Containing an account of the kingdom of
Bow-Woo, in the interior of Africa; with the
climate and natural productions, laws, and
customs peculiar to that place. With an account
of his captivity, sufferings, sales, travels, emancipation,
conversion to the Christian religion,
knowledge of the scriptures, &c. Interspersed
with strictures on slavery, speculative observations
on the qualities of human nature, with
quotation from scripture.

BY BENJAMIN F. PRENTISS, ESQ.

ST. ALBANS, Vt.
PRINTED BY HARRY WHITNEY.
1810.

PREPARED FOR PUBLICATION
BY
HISTORIC PUBLISHING

HISTORIC PUBLISHING
©2017 (Edited Materials)

ISBN: 978-1-946640-69-7

7

INTRODUCTION.

TO THE PUBLIC.

The following sheets contain a general narrative of an African slave; some account of his ancestors, the kingdom of Bow-woo situate on the river Neboah or Niger in the interior of Africa; a description of the soil, climate, vegetables, animals, fowls, fishes, inhabitants, population, government, religion, manners, customs, &c. with a detail of the manner, in which he was kidnapped by the English; a brief account of the custom of civilized nations, in luring the innocent natives of Africa into the net of slavery; and a regular narrative from his own mouth of his captivity, together with many of his native brethren, their sufferings in the prison, or house of subjection, his adventures in the British navy, travels, sufferings, sales, abuses, education, service in the American war, emancipation, conversion to the christian religion, knowledge of the scriptures, memory, and blindness.

WHILE we regret that one innocent man should be held in chains of bondage by another, at any period of time, we must spurn with indignation any idea of the propriety of christian nations, with no other excuse than lust of lucre and difference of religion, holding as slaves, the whole African people, because they are not civilized, or bear not the same complexion, having no other crime, save credulity or innocence.

WHEN we look at the custom of European and American nations, of purchasing, stealing, and decoying into the chains of bondage the negroes of Africa, and that custom sanctioned by the laws of the several governments; that public and private sales are legal; that they are bartered sold, and used as beasts of the field, to the disgrace of civilization, civil liberty, and Christianity; each manly feeling swells with indignation at the horrid spectacle, and whoever have witnessed the miserable and degraded situation to which these unfortunate mortals are reduced, in the West Indies and southern states of United America, must irresistibly be led to ask--Does not civilization produce barbarity? Liberty legalize tyranny? And Christianity deny the humanity it professes?

THIS simple narrative of an individual African cannot possibly compass all the objections to slavery; yet we hope, that the extraordinary features and simplicity of the facts, with the novelty of this publication, will induce many to read and learn the abuses of their fellow beings. If the miserable owner of human blood is not moved to acknowledge the iniquity of his possession, and thereby emancipate his slaves, he will at least alleviate their sufferings.

Within the last century, many sentiments of barbarity and superstition have been done away, "and pure and holy freedom" seems to be verging towards perfection. The Parliament of G. Britain have emancipated their Catholic brethren, the advocates of African freedom have caused the walls of the House of Commons to reverberate the thunder of their eloquence, and a partial emancipation has been effected in their foreign dominions. In America, that spirit of liberty, which stimulated us to shake off a foreign yoke and become an independent nation, has caused the New-England states to emancipate their slaves, and there is but one blot to tarnish the lustre of the American name, which is permitting slavery under a constitution, which declares that "all mankind are naturally and of right ought to be free."

Whoever wishes to preserve the constitution of our general government, to keep sacred the enviable and inestimable principles, by which we are governed, and to enjoy the natural liberty of man, must embark in the great work of exterminating slavery and promoting general emancipation.

THE AUTHOR.

St. Albans, Vt. August, 1810.

CONTENTS OF CHAPTER. 1.

CHAPTER. 1.

FEW indeed have been the travellers who have penetrated into the interior of Africa, as far as the kingdom of Bow-woo, which is situated between the 10th and 20th degrees of north latitude, and between the 6th and 10th of west longitude; and these few have been of that class of travellers, who are either incapable of, or have other pursuits than, communicating to the world that useful information, which has so long been sought in vain. We have indeed obtained some knowledge of the river Neboah or Niger, which runs through' this fertile dominion. According to the account in Morse's Universal Geography, this river is one of the longest in the world. It is said to be navigable for ships of any size, upwards of 1500 miles.

"The Niger, according to the latest accounts, rises near Sankaria, longitude 6 degrees 20 minutes west, latitude 11 deg. north, thence running northerly to Kniabia, thence Northeast to Bammako, thence generally a northeast course to Sego and Jennu, thence, after forming the island of Janbala 90 or 100 miles in length, it leaves Tombuctoo to the north, passes east by Houssa and is lost in the low lands and lakes of Ghana and Wangara; or if we can credit the accounts of Mr. Horneman, it continues its course easterly to the north of the mountains of the Moon; thence northeasterly, until it falls into Bahriel Arrak, which by some has been considered the Nile, from Abyssinia, thence passing Nubia, Sennaar, and Dongolia, it divides Egypt into two parts, pursuing a northerly course, and falls into the Mediterranean by several mouths." But in examining the latest and most approved maps of Africa we cannot find such a river described and it is therefore believed, that no historian or engraver, have been able to delineate exactly the source, or direction of this river. Yet certain it is, that its source is north of the equator, and it is navigable for boats as far as the town of Deauyah, the capital of the kingdom of Bow-woo, which is situated in the county of Hughlough, about three miles from the river on an extensive plain, fertilized by the most luxuriant bounties of nature, peculiar to that clime. According to some writers "this river has its source in the lake Bernu, and runs directly west, enters the Atlantic, or Western Ocean at Senegal, after a course of 2800 miles. It increases and decreases like the Nile, fertilizes the country, and has grains of gold in many parts of it. The Gambia and Senegal are only branches of this river."

In the year 1758, an English vessel, engaged in the slave trade, sailed up this river to the head of navigation; and came to anchor before the town of yellow Bonga. The hurricane months having commenced, they made their peace with the natives, the crew went on shore, and remained through the rainy season, which commences in May and continues until September. After this season of the year was past and during the time of high water, it appears that they continued their passage up the river about 70 miles farther, leaving the Captain, Supercargo, and some other officers and gentlemen to riot in the luxury of the land, with the chief inhabitants, whom their intrigue and apparent affability, the Europeans had induced to become friends. While the vessel lay at anchor in a kind of lake formed in the river, they sent out their boats to steal the innocent natives and succeeded but too well.

Here we will leave these dealers in human flesh and blood, and give some account of the kingdom of Bow-woo, before mentioned. This kingdom, or principality lies about, or the Capital stands about, 280 miles above the town of Yellow Bonga--and here the account is taken from the narrators own mouth who was only 15 or 16 years of age when he was taken and borne away from prosperity, affluence and ease, into ignominious slavery.

This he considers to be a province or colony of the Empire of Morocco, the extent of its boundaries he is unable to ascertain, or can he tell accurately the number of its inhabitants. But the city of Deauyah, the capital and residence of the king, also the native place of Boyrereau, the narrator, is situated on the bank of a small river, about six rods wide, which empties into the Niger, three miles below the town, which is between five and six miles in length, along the east side of said river, and is built in a manner peculiar to that country--the houses are placed in rows, & are joined, only where broken off or intersected by cross streets. This town, besides public buildings, contains nine rows of houses, which are long and low, none more than one story high, except the King's Palace. They are generally built of a kind of clay, made into a cement, which is strengthened by being bound together by small sticks of

14

timber in the body of the walls, so that the face of the same upon both sides is made perfectly smooth and painted, or rather colored white, red, blue, green, purple, or black, according to the fancy of the possessor, which variety renders the view very picturesque and really diverting to the beholder.

The King's palace is situated near the north part of that city, and is composed of about thirty buildings of a very diversified appearance, many of them are in some degree elegant, and this palace includes all the public buildings of the city, except a market and two places of public worship. The country adjacent, for many miles around, appears like a perfect plain, and thinly inhabited, except where there are villages, which are to be met once in about two leagues, generally, in every part of the kingdom, except in the mountainous part, of which he has but little knowledge.-- The climate, as may naturally be supposed, is uniformly hot, except in the rainy seasons, (which is called in their language vauzier) as a very learned writer observes, "The natives in these scorching regions would as soon expect that marble should melt, and flow in liquid streams, as that water, by freezing, should loose its fluidity, be arrested by cold, and ceasing to flow, become like the solid rock."

Laws & Customs peculiar to this Country.

The King is absolute, and enjoys unlimited authority over his People; he has, properly speaking, no ministers: the first grade of nobility, perform the office of counselors of state, and are properly governors or first magistrates in counties, or small districts; and on important occasions, are summoned to sit in grand council before the King.

Petty offences are punished with whipping. Adultery is considered as a capital offence, and the offenders are both tried in grand council before the King, and if clearly proved guilty, by at least two witnesses, both the adulterer and adulteress are buried alive, with their heads above ground, which are shot into pieces, and left exposed to view for the terror of others. Murder and Treason, are adjudged, and punished in the following manner: at the close of a war in which the King in person is commander in chief, he assembles all of his chief officers to what is called the grand War Feast, as a preparatory step to the banquet. He causes strict inquiry to be made into the conduct of every officer and soldier, those who have been guilty of any offence, also those who have signalized themselves, are indiscriminately called before him and his council, on a full, fair and candid investigation. If it does clearly appear, that any officer or soldier, have been guilty of cowardice, they are banished from the kingdom, with this condition, that if they engage in any foreign service, and are once distinguished for their bravery, they are again restored to the privileges of citizenship, but if they return without thus retrieving their characters they are shot as traitors, who are on a fair conviction by two witnesses before the king, in grand council in the foregoing manner, sentenced to be shot

16

by twelve of their ablest archers. Murderers are punished in the same way.

But those who have signalized themselves in battle, or by extraordinary feats of military skill and bravery, or wisdom in the war council, are invited to partake of the feast with the King himself, and created if old men, members of the council; if young men, are made members of the king's life guards, which consists of seventy or eighty young noblemen. This ceremony is performed in the following manner: twelve young virgins of noble birth, are arrayed in blue silk robes, and adorned with gold caps, bracelets of gold upon their right arms and ankles; the hero is seated on a kind of second throne. A maid approaches him with a bowl of water and a white linen cloth, another with a flask of oil, they wash and anoint his feet, he then has a wreath of honor placed upon his head, which is a gold laced cap, with two globes of solid gold on each side, which are for the purpose of fastening in, and supporting plumes by way of ornament; then he is allowed to kiss the queen's hand, and be seated in the proper seat according to his grade of nobility. Thus at the close of a war with the Yough Boo nation, the grandfather of Boyrereau, on the fathers side, was honored with the title of councillor and governor of the county of Hugh Lough, his name was Yarrah Brinch--Here we must observe, that titles in some degree are hereditary as his son, the father of the present narrator, succeeded to the title of governor of said county, whose name was Whryn Brinch: he was also Captain of the kings Life Guards, which as before stated, consisted of Seventy or Eighty men, honored according to the foregoing custom, or descended by right of nobility to this station. His mother's name was Whryn Douden Wrogan, had living, when last he received a father's blessing or beheld a mother's tender anxiety, three Brothers, and four Sisters; to whom the pure and unsullied love of artless simplicity and fraternal affection, rendered thrice dear, as nature unshackled by artifice, was the principle guide of their tender youthful minds; the mention of whose names, calls from a heart almost subdued by grief, one sad tear of fraternal remembrance consecrated to religious resignation. The eldest brother's name was Cressee, 2d Deeyee, 3d Yarrah; the eldest sister's name Desang, 2d Bang, 3d Nabough, 4th Dolacella; Boyrereau descended from Crassee Youghgon, grand-father on the mothers side who was a distinguished officer in a former war, and after a glorious campaign, he returned with the trophies of Victory, covered with wounds to the capital, amid the acclamations of a grateful people, was created first Judge of petty offences, and civil differences, in the county of Voah-Goah; Boyrereau was the third son, and seventh child of an ancient and honorable family, in the kingdom of Bow-woo, situated in that part of Africa called Ethiopia, and of that race of people denominated negroes, whom we as a civilized christian, and enlightened people, presume to call heathen savages, and hold them in chains of bondage, who are our fellow mortals, and children of the same grand-parent of the universe. These reflections bring to his mind the following scripture :--

Ezekiel, chap. 2, ver. 1.--And he said unto me, son of man, stand upon thy feet, and I will speak unto thee.

2. And the spirit entered into me when he spake unto me, and set me upon my feet, that I heard him that spake unto me.

3. And he said unto me, son of man, I send thee to the children of Israel, to a rebellious nation that hath rebelled against me; they and their fathers have transgressed against me, even unto this very day.

4. For they are impudent children, and stiff-hearted: I do send thee unto them; and thou shalt say unto them, Thus saith the Lord God.

5. And they, whether they will hear, or whether they will forbear, (for they are a rebellious house) yet shall know that there hath been a prophet among them.

6. And thou, son of man, be not afraid of them, neither be afraid of their words, though briars and thorns be with thee, and thou dost dwell among scorpions; be not afraid of their words, nor be dismayed at their looks, though they be a rebellious house.

7. And thou shall speak my words unto them, whether they will hear, or whether they will forbear; for they are most rebellious.

8. But thou, son of man, hear what I say unto thee, Be not thou rebellious, like that rebellious house: open thy mouth, and eat that I give thee.

Deuteronomy, chap. 28, ver. 64.--And the Lord shall scatter thee among all people, from the one end of the earth even unto the other; and there thou shalt serve other gods, which neither thou nor thy fathers have known, even wood and stone.

65. And among these nations shalt thou find no case, neither shall the sole of thy foot have rest; but the Lord shall give thee there a trembling heart, and failing of eyes, and sorrow of mind.

66. And thy life shall hang in doubt before thee; and thou shalt fear day and night, and shalt have none assurance of thy life.

67. In the morning thou shalt say, would God it were even! and at even thou shalt say, would God it were morning! For the fear of thine heart where-with thou shalt fear, and for the sight of thine eyes which thou shalt see.

68. And the Lord shall bring thee into Egypt again with ships, by the way whereof I spake unto thee, Thou shalt see it no more again: and there ye shall be sold unto your enemies for bond-men & bond women, & no man shall buy you.

Exodus, chap. 22, ver. 20--He that sacrificeth to any god, save unto the lord only, he shall be utterly destroyed.

21. Thou shalt neither vex a stranger nor oppress him, for ye were strangers in the land of Egypt.

22. Ye shall not afflict any widow, or fatherless child.

23. If thou afflict them in any wise and they cry at all unto me, I will surely hear their cry.

24. And my wrath shall wax hot, and I will kill you with the sword; and your wives shall be widows and your children fatherless.

CONTENTS OF CHAPTER. 2.

CHAPTER. 2.

That the reader may have some idea of the productions of this most luxuriant part of the world, it is thought proper to give an account in this chapter of the various bounties of nature peculiar to this kingdom, which with some small variation is applicable to the whole empire of Morocco, and barbary states, and whoever is in the least acquainted with the history or geography of this quarter of the globe, will at once, see that what is here recorded is undoubtedly true, although it is principally taken from the narrator, and he dependant upon his own memory, and only in the sixteenth year of his age, when he was taken, and in order to demonstrate the strength of his mind and the correctness of his memory, it is thought expedient here to quote from a late modern writer upon the soil, vegetable and animal productions by sea and land, in the states of Barbary. "These states, under the Roman empire; were justly denominated the garden of the world; and to have a residence there was considered as the highest state of luxury. The produce of their soil, formed those magazines, which furnished all Italy, and great part of the Roman empire, with corn, wine and oil. Tho' the lands are now uncultivated, through the oppression and barbarity of their

22

government, yet they are still fertile, not only in the above mentioned commodities, but in dates, figs, raisins, almonds, apples, pears, cherries, plumbs, citrons, lemons, oranges, pomegranates, with plenty of roots and herbs in their kitchen, gardens. Excellent hemp and flax grow on their plains; and by the report of Europeans, who have lived there for some time, the country abounds with all that can add to the pleasures of life; for their great people find means to evade the sobriety prescribed by the Mahometan Law, and make free with excellent wines, and spirits of their own growth and manufacture. Algiers produces salt-petre and great quantities of excellent salt: and lead and iron have been found in several places in Barbary. Neither the Elephant nor the Rhinoceros are to be found in the states of Barbary; but their deserts abound with lions, tigers, leopards, hyenas and monstrous serpents. The Barbary horses were formerly very valuable, and thought equal to the Arabian, though their breed is said now to be decayed, yet some very fine ones are occasionally imported into England. Camels, dromedaries, asses, mules, and also kumrahs, a most serviceable creature, begot by an ass upon a cow, are their beasts of burden. Their cows are but small and barren of milk, their sheep yield indifferent fleeces, but are generally as large as their goats. Bears, porcupines, foxes, apes, hares, rabbits, ferrets, weasels, moles, chameleons, and all kinds of reptiles are found here, besides vermin. (Says Dr. Shaw, speaking of his travels through Barbary) The apprehension we are under, in some parts at least of this country, of being bitten or stung by the scorpion, the viper, or the venomous spider, rarely fail to interrupt our repose, a refreshment so grateful and really necessary to the weary traveller. Partridges, quails, eagles, hawks, and all kinds of wild fowls are found on this coast,

And of the smaller birds, the capsa-sparrow is remarkable for its beauty and the sweetness of its notes, which is thought to exceed that of any bird; but it cannot live out of its own climate. The seas and bays of Barbary abound with the finest and most delicious fish of every kind, and were preferred by the ancients to those of Europe."

Here it may not be improper to digress so far from the narrative, as to give a short sketch of the history of these states, although the kingdom of Bow-woo does not partake much of the general history of them, as it is placed so far in the interior, and bordering upon the negroland, which lies south of this kingdom, therefore it is altogether probable that this part of Africa was never much effected by foreign wars or European conquests, yet as they are now subjects of the empire of Morocco, and must be included among the Barbary states, I think it may be useful to insert the following sketch of the general history of those states, which is quoted from Guthrie's "Geographical, Historical and Commercial Grammar." There perhaps is no problem in history so unaccountable as the decadence of the splendor, power and glory of the states of Barbary, which, when Rome was mistress of the world, formed the fairest jewel in the Imperial diadem. It was not until the seventh century, that after these states had been by turns in the hands of the Vandals and Greek emperors, the Califfs or Saracens of Bagdad conquered them and from thence became masters of almost all Spain, from whence their posterity was totally driven, about the year 1492, when the exiles settled among their friends and countrymen on the Barbary coasts. This naturally begat a perpetual war between them and the Spaniards, who pressed them so hard, that they called to their assistance the two famous

24

brothers, Barbarossa who were admirals of the Turkish fleet, and who, after breaking the Spanish yoke, imposed upon the inhabitants, of all those states, excepting Morocco, their own laws. Some attempts were made by the emperor, Charles the fifth, to redeem Algiers and Tunis, but they were unsuccessful; and as observed, the inhabitants have shaken off the Turkish yoke like wise. The Emperors or Kings of Morocco, are the successors of those sovereigns of that county who are called xeriffs, and whose power resembles that of the caliphate of the Saracens. They have been, in general a set of bloody tyrants; though they have had among them some able princes, particularly Muly Moluc, who defeated and killed Don Sebastian, a king of Portugal. They have lived in almost a continued state of warfare, with the king of Spain and other Christian princes ever since! nor does the crown of Great Britain sometimes disdain, as in the year 1769 to purchase their friendship with presents."

In giving an account of the timber peculiar to this kingdom, we shall mention the name both in the English and Bow-woo languages, that the reader (if a scientific person) may form a correct Idea of the key, or principle, of their tongue; and in tracing some words back to their origin, (Hebrew) from which the narrator considers their language derived, will find him correct; As in their religious belief they have a tradition which has been handed down from time almost immemorial, that all the Ethiopian nations, in short that all Africans descended from Jethro, the priest of Midean.--But more of this hereafter.

The word tree in the Bow-woo language is called Chua or Chuah. Among the names of the trees in his native language, are the autong, or what in english is called red-wool tree; the yahoo, or wool tree, which tree, is productive of wool, but not exactly in imitation either of cotton-wool, or that produced from any kind or breed of sheep known to the narrator. Its qualities, however, are such, that it is capable of being manufactured into cloth, and in that country is very useful, and much used in making a kind of cushion for seats and matrasses, or beds for lodging; also for filling or stuffing the sides and bottoms of their sedan chairs, for the use of the nobility. Naughn chua, or palm tree, which produces most excellent wine, something as our maple in this country produces sugar or molasses, but with much less labor, as the process is almost as simple, and not much unlike tapping the maple, and procuring the sap. The sap or juice of the Palm, when first drawn resembles milk and water, but soon changes its color. Being put into vessels prepared for the purpose, it ferments, and in a few days becomes a most delicious wine. This tree also produces a nut, or fruit, which being pounded, or broken and pressed, makes an oil, which is used as food, or rather as sauce to many kinds of food frequently eaten by the natives, and is often exported to Morocco. Their Divines consider it to possess also a kind of sacred quality, and make use of it to anoint their feet, and the feet of all those whom they consecrate to holiness. The Mahroo-chua, or cabbage tree, which produces clusters of leaves, that form heads, which in size, shape, taste and, color, are almost exactly like our savoy cabbages. The See-chua, or Orange tree, grows in abundance in this country. Their variety and quality of oranges exceed those of any other part of the world. Grossang chua, or lemon tree, is found in every part of the kingdom in great abundance; the produce of which is much superior to any the narrator has seen in any part of the West-Indies. Ossang-chua, or Lime tree, is the natural production of the kingdom of Bow-woo, as also of the adjacent country. There is also a tree peculiar to that country, called in their language the Ahbue-chua, or Bread tree. This tree resembles the pear tree of this country, and produces a fruit, which, when ripe, resembles a bakers loaf of wheat bread, in color, taste, size, and almost in shape, which would rather compare with a pear or red pepper pod This fruit in the season of it, is gathered by the poor class of people, dried and stored in their houses, like our corn, until the next harvest. Augoh chua--no English name known for this tree, as there is no tree in this country which bears it any resemblance, save only the chestnut. It bears a fruit, or rather a nut, about the size of a common hen's egg, and resembles the chestnut in taste and quality, but it is not encompassed within a burr, and is much larger than the chestnut, burr and all. Sigua-chua, or Pomegranate tree, is a natural production of this clime, and is produced in abundance in this kingdom. Douah-chua, or mandrake tree, is peculiar to this part of the world; the fruit resembles a peach, only when ripe it is as blue as what we call blue berry, and is most exquisitely sweet. The mandrake is considered as a royal fruit, and is frequently carried to Morocco to grace their emperor's royal table; and such is the superstition of the natives that they believe it to be a divine, or sacred fruit, and emblematical of the fruit of good works in that promised land "from whose bourne no traveller returns."

Naver-chua, or musk-melon tree which bears a fruit resembling a large ripe musk- melon, in color, shape and size, also in taste, only that it is much sweeter. This fruit is so plenty in the season of it, that not one hundredth part of it can be used, and is suffered to fall and rot upon the ground. The tree resembles the white-wood tree of this country, and grows upon moist land, or near the edge of running water; there is also a kind of stalk grows out of the ground, which is about as big at the bottom as a man's leg, and grows from four to six feet high, that bears a fruit called wheih-whah, or pine-apple. This is thought by some to be a delicious fruit, and a similar kind grows in the West-Indies, and is frequently plenty in our sea-port towns. There is also a tree, or bush, resembling the black alder of America, which bears a plumb, red as scarlet, about the size of a hen's egg, which is exceedingly palatable, and is said to possess all the qualities of meat, bread, and water, which is frequently a sumptuous repast for the forlorn and wearied traveller. *-The name in the language of this kingdom is Zeahhigh.

* NOTE--Mr. Demberger, in his travels in the interior of Africa, makes mention of a kind of fruit he met with at the foot of a mountain, about 250 miles from the river niger, which gave him a delicious meal, as he was almost famished for want of food, having travelled upon the mountains for many days, finding little or no refreshment, which he describes as being red as scarlet, and about the size of a peach. The writer considers this the same mentioned here.

This country, as may well be supposed, produces abundance of Grapes; to mention all of them would swell the description of natural productions into a volume. My object and limits, will necessarily prescribe me on this, as it does on many points, which might be interesting to the botanic reader. Therefore, I will mention only two kinds, which are most extraordinary, and bear no resemblance to the Grapes of any of the European countries; or those produced in any part of the United States of America.

The most curious kind of wine grape, peculiar to this country is the Whahah, or blue grape, which grows on vines in the meadows, or on the banks of slow meandering rivulets, and do not hang in clusters like the English summer or winter grapes, but hang singly, more in imitation of the plumbs, natural to the wilds of Vermont, and many parts of the state of New York; and they are of the size of a common apple, or about two inches in diameter, of a deep blue color, deliciously sweet; the juice is produced in abundance, and when first pressed is exquisitely sweet; but after being kept a few days as naturally might be expected ferments, and has a tartness which gives it a pleasant flavor, especially when required by thirst. The operation upon the faculties of men, is more like that of the real Turkish opium, than any other antidote produced from nature, in the eastern or southern quarters of the globe, yet discovered, (according to the description we receive of it) or explained by any chymist, ancient or modern. The other kind of grape, which we have promised to mention, and which excites our peculiar attention, is called Otua, and is a deep crimson or red grape, the qualities of which are not so well known to the narrator but its peculiar shape and size excite attention, and are so interesting to those who have formed the idea that the very name of grape, in the English language, conveys an idea of a round fruit, produced from a vine, hanging in clusters. The shape of this grape resembles a man's finger; it hangs upon the vine, more like the pods of pole beans, than anything we can conceive; its color resembles blood, its taste the cranberry, and is frequently preserved, and conveyed to the emperor, to add one more foreign dainty to his imperial, diabolical, and tyrannical luxury. There is also a tree in that country, that in leaf, body, shape and size resembles the butternut of this country; its fruit bears some resemblance to the butternut, only its color changes three times; first it is green, next yellow, then when ripe, crimson, and when it begins to decay it becomes a chocolate color, and what is peculiar, there never appears to be any material alteration in the taste or smell.

Thus we end an account of the natural, or spontaneous growth of this country, we have only mentioned a few which are in the fresh recollection of the narrator, and those most extraordinary to American people.

The common productions of art, or the cultivation of the soil, are, first, Morea, or rice, which is similar to that produced in the southern states of United America, and sold in all parts of our common country. Pieree, or corn, which is raised in abundance, almost without the hand of the agriculturalist; as the land is almost completely prepared by nature, and simple sowing, or planting and gathering, is the chief labour to procure an abundant crop. It more resembles the virginia, than what we call indian corn. The Brofea, or barley, is also easily raised, without much labor or attention, and resembles the English barley, which is cultivated some in America, but more in Europe, especially in England. Dra, or Beans, are also raised plentifully. Poah, or pease, are cultivated with ease, and are productive of large crops by being cultivated in the manner they are in America. Cannau, or potatoes, are raised but no other kind than what are called sweet potatoes, which are produced only in our southern climes. Gambreau, or parsnips, are frequently raised or cultivated rather as an ornament to their gardens, than as a necessary vegetable. Threa, or onions, are a sauce which is cultivated with great attention,

30

and considered among the natives as a signal bounty of their great father the sun. Coffee grows almost spontaneously, but is considered as an object of cultivation, and is called, in the Bow-woo language, Leuee.

In mentioning the animals peculiar to this kingdom, we will refer the reader to the natural history of Africa, as it falls not within our limits, or design, to give a particular description of them, and those peculiar to that quarter of the globe will apply with little, or no variation, to this kingdom. Therefore, we will only give the names in both languages, of such as the narrator can recollect. Zenamah, or Lyon; Wallah, or Leopard; Sopeah, or Horse; Oblea, or Cow, Douo, or cattle; Bleah, or sheep. There are two kinds of Goats, to be met here; the one, the large kind, which is called bowh, the small goat is called Auvaun. It produces milk, although the cow does not; neither do the sheep produce wool. The animal in this country, which is commonly called Oran-Outang, is known by the name of Yeahoo. Monkies are extremely plenty in every part of this dominion, and are called Auzee. They are a very imitative animal, but more peculiarly so, in this part of the world, than in any other, as those children of nature give them lessons of imitation, more striking, as more natural, than do the Europeans, where art has almost defaced the beauties, which once adorned a primitive world. The Auyeury, or what we call baboons, are met with in abundance in the interior of the country. The camel is called in the Bow-woo Language Auwolah, and is very useful to the natives, particularly in their wars, and journeys to Morocco. The Unicorn is a noble animal, and a native of that part of the world. They are dangerous in case of resentment, and are called by the name of Beauch. Among the mountains they

31

frequently find Panthers, but their name in his native language, the narrator has forgotten. There are several kinds of squirrels in this country, but much smaller in size than the grey or black squirrel of America; none being larger than the red squirrel of Vermont, and are called in their language esujah.

There are several kinds of amphibious quadrupeds in this country. An animal resembling the North American beaver in shape and size, is frequently met in the low lands and upon the banks of rivers. The Africans call it, Zoo-row, it is of a blue color, they make but little account of it, as the furr is indifferent, and the flesh is not used by the natives, but it provides for itself with as much sagacity as the beaver of this country; it fells trees, and builds shelters partly above and partly in the water, so as to be capable of shunning an attack, either from sea or land. Thus fortified, he defies the king of the forest, or aquatic foe, unless they, contrary to nature, should enter into a coalition. The Vro roo, is an amphibious animal, resembling the musk-rat, only its adroitness is unequalled by any other animal, known in that country. It is said to plunge into the water, on one side of a stream that is ten rods in width, and in ten seconds appears upon the opposite side, and seems rather to dart than run until it is out of reach of the foe. The Vro-roo is a very inoffensive animal, and appears to fear every creature that approaches it. There are many frogs, toads, crockadiles, serpents and vipers, The alligators are said to resemble those of South America, and are sometimes the destroyers of children. The turtles or terrapins, are exceedingly plenty; many are of a monstrous size, and are called Slough-Lough; they are taken for the purpose of making use of their shells, which are frequently used as boats, or scows, in their small streams.

Fowls are numerous--however my limits will not permit me to mention but few. There is the Autorouk, or wild turkey, very numerous and useful. The Gay, or Partridge, bears a great likeness to the partridges among us. The Whetece, or goose, more resembles the wild goose, than our domestic or English goose. The Proseau, or hawks, are of various kinds and sizes. The Soo, or hen, resembles the guinea-hen, frequently seen in America, and is undoubtedly of the same species. There are also Fleuhie, or eagles, of a monstrous size, that are dangerous to children in many parts of the kingdom. They, however, build their nests upon the mountains, among the rocks, and seldom, unless driven by hunger, or in pursuit of food for their young, descend upon the low lands, where it is thick settled. They have been taken when young and kept as a curiosity, and at two years old weighed 160 pounds. Their backs are a dark blue or black, with white talons and breasts.

It may be said no country abounds with a greater variety of birds, of various kinds, which it is impossible to give a general description of. The aquatic animals, or fishes, peculiar to this country, are not very numerous, as none are presumed to inhabit this interior country, only such as came up the river Niger. The name of fish is called Threa.--I shall mention only two kinds; the one prized very high by the natives, resembles the sturgeons frequently taken in our rivers; they are frequently taken and offered up as sacrices for the sins of the people. Also, they always have a dish cooked at the feast of the Passover, which will be mentioned hereafter. There is an excellent fish, which the narrator has forgotten the African name of, yet the English of it signifies gold fish, it is about the size of our salmon, and is covered with scales that are transparent, and the same color of pure gold----they are taken in abundance, and sold in the capital by the poorer class of people, many of whom follow fishing for a subsistence.

Here we close our account of the various natural productions of this kingdom; many by design have been omitted, as an account of them might not be amusing to but few readers, and many have been unavoidably left out, as the narrator could not recollect their names in his original tongue or native language. Extraordinary as some facts may appear there can be no doubt of their authenticity, and when we consider that both ancient and modern authors have agreed that, by nature, Africa abounds with more spontaneous luxuries than any other quarter of the globe; which tends to make man indolent and barbarous. Yet the peculiar characteristic of this nation, is peace, humanity and courtesy, to strangers.

There is a custom that is strictly adhered to in all parts of the kingdom, that is, if a stranger comes among them, of whatever nation or description, and makes inquiry for any person, the person enquired of is obliged to wash and anoint the strangers feet, give him refreshment, if required, and either go with him to the person, if known to the native, or give him the best directions in his power, and on refusing or neglecting to do the same, on complaint and conviction, the offender must be publicly whipped twenty-five stripes. However absurd or ridiculous this custom may appear to a civilized people, certain it is fraught with courtesy and benevolence; and if we could find the same spirit prevalent among a christian people, what a good thing it would be in the estimation of the stranger who should receive the benefit, and he could exclaim with the Psalmist.

Psalm CXXXIII.

The benefit of the communion of Saints.

A song of degrees of David.

1. Behold, how good and how pleasent it is for brethren to dwell together in unity.

2. It is like the precious ointment upon the head, that ran down upon the beard, even Aaron's beard; that went down to the skirts of his garments;

3. As the dew of Hermon, and as the dew that descended upon the mountains of Zion, for there the Lord commanded the blessing, even life forevermore.

Psalm CXXVIII.

The sundry blessings which follow them that fear God.

A song of degrees.

1. Blessed is every one that feareth the Lord; that walketh in his ways.

2. For thou shalt eat the labor of thy hands: happy shalt thou be, and it shall be well with thee.

3. Thy wife shall be as a fruitful vine by the sides of thine house: thy children like olive-plants round about thy table.

4. Behold, that thus shall the man be blessed that feareth the Lord.

5. The Lord shall bless thee out of Zion and thou shalt see the good of Jerusalem all the days of thy life.

6. Yea, thou shalt see thy children's children, and peace upon Israel.

The narrator feels the full force of the application of the following psalm to himself, and hopes all those who are advocates of a difference in human nature, or for slavery, will read.

PSALM 129.

1. Many a time have they afflicted me from my youth, may Isreal now say,

2 Many a time have they afflicted me from my youth; yet they have not prevailed against me.

3. The plowers plowed upon my back, they made long their furrows.

4. The Lord is righteous: he hath cut asunder the cords of the wicked.

5. Let them all be confounded and turned back that hate Zion.

6. Let them be as the grass upon the house tops, which withereth afore it groweth up;

7. Wherewith the mower filleth not his hand, nor he that bindeth sheaves his bosom.

8. Neither do they which go by, say, The blessing of the Lord be upon you we bless you in the name of the Lord.

CONTENTS OF CHAPTER. 3.

CHAPTER. 3.

In the year 1758 Whryn Brinch was summoned to attend the King on a tour to the city of Morocco to visit the Emperor, as was the custom to be performed or a duty imposed upon them each year, this being the first year that Whryn Brinch commanded the King's life guards on a tour to the western or Atlantic ocean; of course had little or no knowledge of such a being as a white Man; and had as imperfect an idea of a ship or vessel as he would have of anything that was in existence.

In this tour the Father of the narrator purchased a pair of pistols and piece of purple silk, and on his return, while enjoying the pleasure of the society of his growing family, all rejoicing at his return from so long and arduous a journey, and their curiosity not a little excited by the articles of European and India manufacture which he had presented them with. While my Father and Mother had some gentle dispute about the quality of the silk (for here the writer takes the language of the narrator) I was busy snapping and observing the beauties of the pistol. As soon as an opportunity offered I asked my father where the pistols came from, and where he had obtained them, he said, they came from the white people, who lived on the waters, and came to our shores and landed at Morocco, where he purchased them. White people! said I, what kind of beings are they? How do they get to Morocco, from the great waters? Why, said my father, they have every appearance of men, like our people only they are as pale as the moon, and are covered with clothes from head to foot, with large platforms upon their heads; and they float along on high shells like the Slough Barrow, * only one shell contains hundreds of them, and it has wings like the Ethelry. **

* Slough Borrow, is in the English language, Turtle or Terrapin.

** Ethelry, is Needle or Spindle, which have wings and hover or light upon the water at pleasure

Much more was said, but my attention was so taken up with the pistols, that I have forgotten the remainder, the conversation soon turned upon the feast dedicated to the sun, (which is performed something in imitation of the feast of the Passover we read of) which was fast approaching, and is always celebrated at this season of the year. And here I will observe the king always performs his journey to the Emperor's castle during the rainy season, as in any other season of the year, it is dangerous to pass the great deserts of sand which lie between Deau-Yah and Morocco; and the feast commences immediately on the king's return. While domestic joy gladdened the heart of each individual of our artless and innocent family, and the public mind of the whole nation was occupied with preparations, and the anticipated felicity which would gladden the hearts of every individual of the community; little did I think of my approaching fate. No favorite genius whispered to me impending destruction, or years of ignominious slavery; little did I foresee that when I should be raised to the zenith of all earthly enjoyment, that in a moment I should become a slave.

The feast approached, and the preparations were complete on the part of my father, who was to be mounted upon an elegant African horse, clothed in a beautiful scarlet net, which he had procured at Morocco, he to be clothed in a purple silk dress, according to the style of the moors, with his pistols hanging by his sides, fastened to a leather girdle of scarlet; with a cap laced with gold, with two globes of solid gold on each side, large enough to fasten in twelve plumes, by way of ornament. Thus prepared, in the morning my father assembled his whole family, before the rising of the sun, to invoke his blessing. After the usual ceremonies of invocation, homage and adoration, the whole family sat down to breakfast, a frugal repast of milk and fruit, with hearts alive to filial and fraternal affection. Reciprocal pleasure crowned the board with the purest domestic delight.

The king's trumpet sounded; the escort appeared; my father mounted his steed and was away, to obey the commands of the king, and enjoy the pleasure of the feast-- which is performed in the following manner.--At sunrise the king and his nobles assemble upon a large plain, the king, queen, and some of the noble ladies of honor are with the high priests, ushered into the center, while the remaining nobility and gentry form a large circle with the king's life guard, between him and the rising sun; then a circle of light-horse is formed, next the armies of the nation, which is completed with the indiscriminate multitude of every sex and age. As soon as bright Sol makes his appearance in the east, the trumpets are sounded from one end of the plain to the other. A solemn dirge is chanted, in the style of a requiem of an old catholic abby, by the females of honor, together with the priestesses, who hold a conspicuous rank among the nobility. There are certain ceremonies performed in the meantime, by the royal and divine personages, such as offering up sacrifices according to the custom of the Jews. Lambs, kids, gold-fishes, mandrakes and scarlet grapes, are offered up as sacrifices to their God, the Sun, whom they worship as devoutly as Christians worship the trinity. After this solemn devotion ends, the king, with his life-guards in front, forms a procession; the oldest and highest in rank of his nobility form in next to him, with the divines in front of them, who always hold a conspicuous rank among the favorites of the government, on account of their divinity. Next, the young men of noble birth and titles form. When the armies of the nations are formed in a manner peculiar to this tribe, or kingdom, the light dragoons form in front of the armed forces; then the infantry, or footmen, are formed in ranks according to their grades in the field. To close the procession, the multitude of every sex and age are formed on, according to their seniority. The whole procession is abundantly supplied with the best of instrumental music, such as trumpets, drums, fifes, flutes, tambourines, violins and many other instruments peculiar to the country, the

African names of which I have forgotten. They march, as formed, in circles, in imitation of the sun, who, in their opinion, passes around them to examine their actions, during which ceremony, they play, sing, dance and shout from one end of the procession to the other, which induces me to believe that this people descended from the children of Israel, as when Josiah kept the feast of the Passover, for the dedication of the temple, he caused the chief priests and disciples or principals, to form in circles around him, and the multitude formed a large circle around the temple, which in this manner with certain ceremonies was dedicated to the God of Israel.

And having received, through the blessings of divine providence, a partial English education, although' a poor African Slave, who are shunned and despised by a paler race of Christian people; I have presumed to read, understand, believe and expound, the scriptures, as the oracles of divine inspiration.

We read in sacred writ that Adam was the first man, and Eve the first woman, created by God, in his own likeness, perfect, and placed in the garden of Eden, from whom descended all human beings, then where is the distinction? Being so placed, they were irresistibly drawn by the involuntary volition of their own wills to partake of the forbidden fruit, for it was God's will, and that was irresistible. They could have no foretaste, or desire, but their maker's, therefore it was involuntary; it was by the lure of the serpent and design of their creator; yet they being perfectly free it must be the volition of their own wills, that they did thus partake of the forbidden fruit, which produced the knowledge of good and evil; corrupted the whole human race, and damned all mankind without any possible redemption, save only through the mercy of god himself. Adam, Eve, and their descendants, we have a regular history of, in the four first books of the holy bible, down to the Israelites nation. Moses, the leader of the children of Israel, and the inspired author of the sacred history, here mentioned, it appears, married the daughter of Jethro, the priest of Midian.

Now, although I am a poor, despised black wretch, in the sight of man, permit me, kind reader, to offer some ideas of mine, and do not despise them because they come from an African negro, who are, by white men, considered an inferior race of beings. I, although' thus considered of an inferior race, do hope, and verily believe, that I have received that blessing promised to those who have faith in God, and continue to the end in ways of well doing. Therefore, I have occasion to reflect upon the scriptures, according to which I find that there were flags set up to prevent my soul from entering the garden of Eden, after Adam and Eve were driven out; and that they had no children until after that time. And we, in the sacred description of the place, read that there was a river running out of the same, which had four heads. This I understand to be a figurative description of the world, or globe, which is inhabited by man. The first branch of this river is called Pison: Genesis ii--10.--And a river went out of Eden to water the garden: and from thence it was parted, and became into four heads.

11. The name of the first is Pison: that is it which compasseth the whole land of Havilah, where there is gold.

12. And the gold of that land is good: there is bdellium and the onyx stone.

13. and the name of the second is Gihon: the same is it that compasseth the whole land of Ethiopia.

14. And the name of the third river is Hiddekel: that is it which goeth toward the east of Assyrria. And the fourth river is Euphrates.

Now, as that part of the globe called Africa, is productive of much gold, I am led to form this idea, that the river Pison is emblematical of that quarter which is figuratively set forth as the land of Havillah, and being ranked as first in scripture, where do we find a reason to believe the inhabitants are an inferior race of beings? Some of the divine advocates for slavery, presume to say, that the negroes descended from Cain, who was cursed, and had a mark put upon him; that all his descendant are natural born slaves. Was not the mark to prevent his being hurt, or at least killed; if so, what can our christian readers say to the conduct of slave owners, who whip, scourge and put to death the poor african negro, considering them as descendants of cain. But pursue this point a little farther: Genesis, iv--25--And Adam knew his wife again, and she bare a son and called his name Seth; for God, said she, hath appointed me another seed instead of Abel, whom Cain Slew.

26. And to Seth, to him also there was born a son, and he called his name Enos: then began men to call upon the name of the Lord.

From Seth we have a regular genealogy of the Patriarchs, down to Noah, who had three sons, Shem, Ham and Japheth, who took to themselves wives, and entered the ark with their father, and all the rest of the world were drowned in the flood, except Noah and his wife, his three sons and their wives; then where are the descendants of Cain?----Gen. vii--9--And Noah went in, and his sons, and his wife, and his sons' wives with him, into the ark, because of the waters of the flood.

21. And all flesh died that moved upon the earth, both of fowl, and of cattle, and of beasts, and of every creeping thing that creepeth upon the earth, and every man.

22. All in whose nostrils was the breath of life, of all that was in the dry land died.

Now let the advocates for a distinction in qualities of human nature, ponder well upon the foundation of their arguments, if they believe the scripture.--But to turn to the feast at Deau-Yah.----The next ceremony was, the feast or banquet which was prepared in a kind of festoon, upon the side of the plain. Where nature had been in the least deficient in the production of natural shade, art was made use of to supply that deficiency! and a complete canopy of ever-green, shaded all those who were seated at the banquet. The repast is frugal and chiefly composed of the natural productions of the country with the aid of little or no art in the preparation; dates, figs, plumbs, grapes, goats milk, cream, gold-fish, palm wine and oil, are the chief dishes that comprise the sumptuous feast. As soon as they rise from their refreshment, which seldom detains them more than thirty minutes, the trumpets sound, and they repair, in the beforementioned order, to the king's palace, where he is seated upon the throne in an open porch of the palace, fronting the lawn; when all are seated he suffers a gay and warlike tune to be sung and played by his subjects of all ranks; this is generally in praise of his emperor or of himself. When the music ceases, he delivers, in person, a speech, during which time the most profound silence is observed. At the close of which he calls in the aid of a few of his chief councillors, and appoints all the officers, or governors of towns, counties and districts; fills all vacancies as far as can be done until the setting of the sun, at which time all business ceases, solemn music strikes up and lasts for about five minutes, which closes by the sound of the trumpet, and firing of platoons, at which signal the exercises of the day cease, and all retire to enjoy, without ceremony, such enjoyment as is preferred. Thus the feast continues from day to day, until all the officers of the government are appointed and installed, or sworn into office, the pleasures varying from day to day. One day, combats are performed; next, feats of agility; on another, acts of strength &c. until the feast closes, which continues generally about seven days. There is a tradition which was handed down among us, that this custom was anciently introduced by a great high priest of a foreign land, whose name was Ziphia; and here I will observe that there are certain societies, as I was informed by my Grandmother, Whryn Dooden Wrogan, which had certain oral information communicable to each other on certain obligations being taken, which traced the origin of that people to the days of Noah, who, according to divine history, with his sons, Shem, Ham and Japheth, are the second original fathers of all human beings. Ziphia the high priest in our language, I understand to be Jethro, the priest

46

of Midian, who went and lived in a foreign land, and who was father in law to Moses, and O! how my soul has regretted that I was too young to become a member of the before mentioned society, for there, I verily believed I should learn the origin of all nations; the veil of superstition would be rent in twain. Man, in his native elements would be held to view; their origin and descent would be portrayed; each kingdom and nation would be clearly seen and known, if real distinctions are; the proofs would be strong and convincing; if all mankind were naturally equal, we, however sable, if wise and virtuous, should be on a level with all mankind. These things bring to my mind a chapter of sacred scripture which I often repeat, when memory brings me back to my native land; the visions of night cause me to read, while in the arms of Morpheus, the following scripture, which is verified by the ancient customs of my forefathers.

EXODOUS, Chap. 18.

1. Jethro bringeth to Moses his wife and two sons: 7. Moses entertaineth him, 13. and accepteth his counsel.

1. When Jethro the priest of Midian, Moses' father-in-law, heard of all that God had done for Moses, and for Israel his people, and that the Lord had brought Isral out of Egypt;

2. Then Jethro, Moses' father-in-law, took Zipporah, Moses wife, after he had sent her back.

3. And her two sons, of which the name of the one was Gershom; (for he said, I have been an alien in a strange land;)

4. And the name of the other was Eliezer; (for the God of my father, said he, was mine help, and delivered me from the sword of Pharaoh:)

5. And Jethro, Moses' father-in-law, came with his sons and his wife unto Moses into the wilderness, where he encamped at the mount of God:

6. And he said unto Moses, I, thy father in law, Jethro, am come unto thee, and thy wife, and her two sons with her.

7. And Moses went out to meet his father-in-law, and did obeisance and kissed him; and they asked each other of their welfare: and they came into the tent.

8. And Moses told his father-in-law all that the Lord had done unto Pharaoh, and to the Egyptians, for Israel's sake, and all the travail that had come upon them by the way, and how the Lord delivered them.

9. And Jethro rejoiced for all the goodness which the Lord had done to Israel, whom he had delivered out of the hand of the Egyptians.

10. And Jethro said, blessed be the Lord who hath delivered you out of the hand of the Egyptians.

11. Now I know that the Lord is greater than all gods: for in the thing wherein they dealt proudly, he was above them.

12. And Jethro, moses father-in-law, took a burnt offering and sacrifices for God: and Aaron came, and all the elders of Israel, to eat bread with Moses' father-in-law, before God.

13. And it came to pass on the morrow that Moses sat to judge the people; and the people stood by Moses from the morning unto the evening.

14. And when Moses' father-in-law saw all that he did to the people, he said, what is this thing that thou doest to the people? why sittest thou thyself alone, and all the people stand by thee from morning unto even?

15. And Moses said unto his father-in-law, Because the people come unto me to enquire of God.

16. When they have a matter they come unto me, and I judge between one and another; and I do make them know the statutes of God, and his laws.

17. And Moses' father-in-law said unto him, The thing that thou doest is not good.

18. Thou wilt surely wear away, both thou and this people that is with thee: for this thing is too heavy for thee; thou art not able to perform it thyself, alone.

19. Hearken now unto my voice, I will give thee counsel, and God shall be with thee. Be thou for the people to Godward, that thou mayest bring the causes unto God:

20. And thou shalt teach them ordinances and laws, and shalt shew them the way wherein they must walk, and the work they must do.

21. Moreover thou shalt provide out of all the people, able men, such as fear God, men of truth, hating covetousness; and place such over them, to be rulers of thousands, and rulers of hundreds, rulers of fifties and rulers of tens.

22. And let them judge the people at all seasons: and it shall be, that every great matter they shall bring unto thee; but every small matter they shall judge; so shall it be easier for thyself, and they shall bear the burden with thee.

23. If thou shalt do this thing, and God command thee so, then thou shalt be able to endure, and all this people shall also go to their place in peace.

54. So Moses hearkened to the voice of his fateer-in-law, and did all that he had said.

25. And Moses chose able men out of all Israel, and made them heads over the people, rulers of thousands, rulers of hundreds, rulers of fifties and rulers of tens.

26. And they judged the people at all seasons: the hard causes they brought unto Moses, but every small matter they judged themselves.

27. And Moses let his father-in-law depart; and he went his way into his own land.

At the close of the feast the Boys of the partakers there of, as is the custom, were allowed to put on some conspicuous ornament of their fathers and go to such amusements as they thought most pleasing to their propensities, bathing in the Neboah or Niger, being considered a useful as well as pleasing amusement. On the close of the feast, myself with thirteen of my comrades, went down to the great Neboah to bathe--this was in the 16 year of my age; my father and mother delighted in my vivacity and agility; on this occasion, every exertion on their part seemed to be made use of, to gratify, what they called, their youthful Boy. As it was almost a league and an half, everything was done for my outset, whether at the time I was convinced, or whether by infatuation, I have convinced myself from events, that there was something portentous in my parting from my parents, I am unable to say. But it appears to me now that their whole souls were extacy in thus gratifying their darling boy, all was hilarity, anxiety, and delight; my mother pressed me to her breast, and warned me of the dangers of the waters, for she knew no other. My brothers and sisters all assisted to ornament me and give me advice, and wish me much delight. My father with the Austerity of a Judge, tenderly took me by the hand, and said, my son conduct yourself worthy of me, and here you shall wear my cap; he then put it upon my head, and said, My dear Boyrereau, do not get drowned, but return before the setting of our great father the sun. My comrades were waiting at the porch of our front door, I flew to the door, with a heart lighter than a feather; My brothers and sisters followed my father and mother, standing behind them to observe my departure and agility, O! God that my limbs had refused their office on that fatal day, or I had been laid a corpse on the clay of my native land, before I had been suffered to move from the threshold of my father's dwelling. O! the day that I passed the church for the last time, a whole family following with anxious looks my steps and motion, the well-known sportive rivulet, I passed the arch of clay. I, before I descended the hill which shut me from the sight of home forever cast behind me one last and longing look to see if I could catch one pleasing glance of a fond mother; but alas! I could discover no trace of home, only the pleasing and conspicuous views of my native town. When I turned round, I found my companions before me. The anticipated sport, caused my heart to leap with joy, I ran down the declivity of the hill, we reached the Neboah; about 10 o'clock in the morning, we went down upon a point or rather elbow of the river, just above the junction of the small river before mentioned with the Niger.

There was a small shade of grape vines under which there was a smooth flat of green grass, we quickly and hastily undressed ourselves and prepared for the consummation of our wishes; kings upon their thrones might envy our felicity. As we could anticipate no greater pleasure, and knew no care. A perfect union prevailed; all had a noble emulation to excel in the delightful sport before us; we plunged into the stream, dove, swam, sported and played in the current; all striving to excel in feats of activity, until wearied with the sport, we returned to the shore, put on some of our clothing, began to think about returning to our homes, as fatigue and hunger invited.

When we ascended the bank, to our astonishment we discovered six or seven animals fastening a boat, and immediately made towards us. Consternation sat fixed upon every brow, and fear shook every frame; each member refused its office. However, home invited so urgently, that nature began to do her duty, we flew to the wood with precipitation. But Lo! when we had passed the borders and entered the body thereof, to our utter astonishment and dismay, instead of pursuers we found ourselves waylaid by thirty or forty more of the same pale race of white Vultures, whom to pass was impossible, we attempted without deliberation to force their ranks. But alas! we were unsuccessful, eleven out of fourteen were made captives, bound instantly, and notwithstanding our unintelligible entreaties, cries & lamentations, were hurried to their boat, and within five minutes were on board, gagged, and carried down the stream like a sluice; fastened down in the boat with cramped jaws, added to a horrid stench occasioned by filth and stinking fish; while all were groaning, crying and praying, but poor creatures to no effect. I after a siege of the most agonizing pains describable, fell into a kind of torpid state of insensibility which continued for some hours. Towards evening I awoke only to horrid consternation, deep wrought misery and woe, which defies language to depict. I was pressed almost to death by the weight of bodies that lay upon me; night approached and for the first time in my life, I was accompanied with gloom and horror.

Thus in the 16th year of my age, I was borne away from native innocence ease, and luxury, into captivity, by a christian people, who preach humility, charity, and benevolence. "Father! forgive them for they know not what they do."

I remained in this situation about four days, the cords had cut the flesh, I was much bruised in many parts of my body, being most of the time gagged, and having no food only such as those brutes thought was necessary for my existence. Sometimes I courted death, but home would force upon me with all its delights and hope, that soother of all afflictions taught me to bear with patience my present sufferings.

CONTENTS OF CHAPTER. 4.

Arrival at the vessel--met 30 or 40 more slaves--their condition--scripture--first night of confinement--description of the captain--feast on board--the inhabitants of the town of Yellow-Bonga kidnapped--the manner of confinement on board account of an Englishman, who had married the princess of Guinguina--his treaty with her father--our departure--incidents on our passage--arrival at Barbadoes--Cyneyo's speech, in the house of subjection--the captain's answer--manner of living, &c.

CHAPTER 4.

ON the fourth day, about four o'clock, in the afternoon we arrived at the ship, and were carefully taken out of the boat, and put on board; even this momentary relief seemed to cheer my desponding spirits, and at least eased the pains I endured, by relieving me of those galling cords with which I was bound. I was suffered to walk upon the deck for a few minutes under a strong guard, which gave my blood an opportunity in some degree to assume its usual circulation. But in a short time I was forced into the hole, where I found my comrades, with about thirty more poor African wretches whom the ships crew had stolen from a neighboring tribe. These poor creatures were screaming, crying and wringing their hands, with prayers and ejaculations to the great Father for their deliverance. This group was composed of men, women and children, some little girls and boys, not more than six or seven years of age were shut up in a pen or stye, crying for food and water and their fathers and mothers. One little boy about seven years of age, told me he went in the evening to drive the goats for his mother, and they ran after him and caught him, and his mother did not know where he was, and he was afraid his little brothers and sisters would starve, as he was the oldest child and there was no one to drive the goats, as his father was taken away before, therefore there was no one to help her now.

The author has inserted the following lines, taken from a periodical publication, of 1804, which he deems pathetic and apropos.

"Help! Oh, help! thou God of Christians!
Save a mother from despair!
Cruel white men steal my children!
God of Christians hear my prayer!

From my arms by force they're sever'd;
Sailors drag them to the sea;
Yonder ship, at anchor riding,
Swift will carry them away.

There my son lies stripped and bleeding;
Fastwith thongs his hands are bound;
See the tyrants how they scourge him;
See his sides a reeking wound!

See his little sister by him;
Quaking, trembling, how she lies!
Drops of blood her face be sprinkle;
Tears of anguish fill her eyes.

Now they tear her brother from her,
Down below the deck he's thrown.
Stiff with beating, thro' fear silent,
Save a single death like groan.

Hear the little creature begging;
"Take me white men for your own!
Spare! Oh, spare my darling brother!
He's my mothers only son."

See, upon the shore she's raving,
Down she falls upon the sands:
Now she tears her flesh with madness
Now she prays with lifted hands.

"I am young, and strong, and hardy,
He's a sick and feeble boy;
Take me, whip me, chain me, starve me
All my life I'll toil with joy.

Christians, whose the God you worship,
Is he cruel, fierce or good?
Does he take delight in mercy?
Or in spilling human blood?
Ah my poor distracted mother!
Hear her scream upon the shore:"--
Down the savage captain struck her,
Lifeless on the vessel's floor.

Up his sails he quickly hoisted,
To the ocean bent his way;
Headlong plung'd the raving mother,
From a high rock in the sea."

I for a moment forgot my distress, and shed one tear for the boy. But sympathy assumed her dominion, and we all wept for one another and ourselves; the children crying for bread and water, and no white soul paid any attention.

MATTHEW, VII----7.

7. Ask, and it shall be given you; seek and ye shall find; knock and it shall be opened unto you:

8. For every one that asketh, receiveth; he that seeketh, findeth; and to him that knocketh, it shall be opened.

9. Or what man is there of you, who, if his son ask bread, will he give him a stone?

10. Or if he ask a fish, will he give him a serpent?

11. If ye then, being evil, know how to give good gifts unto your children, how much more shall your father, which is in heaven, give good things to them that ask him?

12. Therefore all things whatsoever ye would that men should do to you, do ye even so to them: for this is the law and the prophets.

25. And, behold, a certain lawyer stood up, and tempted him, saying. Master, what shall I do to inherit eternal life?

26. He said unto him, What is written in the law? how readest thou?

27. And he, answering, said, Thou shalt love the lord, with all thy heart, and with all thy soul, and with all thy strength, and with all thy mind; and thy neighbor as thyself.

28. And he said unto him, Thou hast answered right: this do, and thou shalt live.

29. But he, willing to justify himself, said unto Jesus, And who is my neighbor?

30. And Jesus, answering, said, a certain man went down from Jerusalem to Jericho, and fell among thieves, which stripped him of his raiment, and wounded him, and departed, leaving him half dead.

31. And by chance there came down a certain priest that way; and when he saw him he passed by on the other side.

32. And likewise a Levite, when he was at the place, came and looked on him and passed by on the other side.

33. But a certain Samaritan, as he journeyed, came where he was: and when he saw him, he had compassion on him,

34. And went to him and bound up his wounds, pouring in oil and wine, and set him on his own beast, and brought him to an inn, and took care of him.

35. And on the morrow, when he departed, he took out two pence, and gave them to the host, and said unto him, take care of him; and whatsoever thou spendest more, when I come again I will repay thee.

36. Which now of these three, thinkest thou, was neighbor unto him that fell among the thieves?

37. And he said, He that shewed mercy on him. Then said Jesus unto him, Go, and do thou likewise.

As I walked round, I observed some men & women in the hatchway, in Irons; they were pleading for their deliverance, or that they rather than remain as they were, might receive instant death; what had been their offence I never learned. At sun down we were separated into small parties, and I was separated from my comrades, and bolts and bars for the first time in my life confined me to a small apartment, and language cannot describe more misery than I experienced that night. Solitude brought home to my tender, youthful mind, remembrance and reflection, two unwelcome messengers. But early next morning, all was bustle, noise and confusion; they weighed anchor, hoisted sail, and we sailed down the river; here to my sorrow I learned what the white men came to Morocco in, which my father before had so imperfectly described to me, on his last return home. In a short time we came to anchor before a town called in my language, Yellow Bonga the English name of which place I could never learn.

As before observed, the captain, super-cargo, and many of the English gentlemen had been residents in this town for many months during their stay here they had ingratiated themselves with the natives, whose credulity taught them to believe that they were as honest and innocent as the natives were themselves, the ship lay before this place for some days during which time there was much passing and re-passing. One day a man came on board, whom they paid particular, reference to, who afterwards, I learned, was the commander himself. He was about five feet two inches in height, duck legged, high shoulders and hollow backed, his hair being red as scarlet, cued down his back, to his hips, which were broad and prominent, his nose aquiline, high cheek bones, with a face about the color of what we call crimson grapes, but what is more familiar to our ideas his complexion, was that of a red beat his nose eclipsed it, his eyes resembled a bowl of cream in a smoky house sprinkled with white ashes and hemlock tan with a chin that defied them to examine his laced vest which encompassed a huge paunch, that would astonish a Bishop, or host of a London porter house; his mouth had destroyed about one third of his face, and each wing was about attacking his ears, with ammunition within, called teeth, that represented gourd seeds, his lips were about the thickness of the blade of a case knife & appeared as if they had been at variance for many years, for the barrier between them bid defiance to an union; his hat resembled a triangle being cocked in the ancient mode, with three sharp corners, brim laced with gold, and gold laced loops. Time had made some impression upon its former beauty; but the ostentation of the wearer made up all deficiencies; but the description is tedious, all things corresponded; yes, his mind agreed with his appearance, and his dress was emblematical of his feelings, which were bedaubed with iniquity and grown very stale.

We had not remained many days, in this situation before we learned by the Interpreter, that the officers were courting some of the women, and were almost idolized by the natives, who were making public feasts for their amusement, and entertainment. At length it was announced that a grand feast was to be held on board of the ship; apparent preparations, were made accordingly, and all the principal inhabitants of the Town were to attend. This was considered as a civility due from that deluded people, to the officers of the vessel, while the blackest perfidy rankled in the hearts of those traitorous villains, who conceived and executed the plot. A general invitation was accordingly given to all classes, without distinction. The day arrived, the boats of the ship were busily employed in bringing on board the visitors. The principal inhabitants of the Town came on board; in short, but few stayed behind only the sick, lame, aged and children; they brought with them many valuable articles of plate, &c. when all were on board, the festivity commenced, but mark, the slaves were cautiously concealed in the cockpit, that vigilance might be kept asleep and suspicion lulled into security. When they had regaled themselves with Food, Brandy, Spirits and Wine, were introduce and prepared in many ways to make it the more delicious. When they had drank freely, laudanum was secretly conveyed into their liquor, a general intoxication, and sound sleep soon prevailed, and insensibility was the consequence. These dexterous dealers in iniquity seized upon the moment, fastened with implements already prepared, each individual down upon their backs, with poles across their breasts and legs, with hands and feet drawn up by cords to certain loop holes therein. In this situation they are obliged to lie during a six months voyage, fed like hogs in the stye by their drivers. Their excrement however was taken out by women and sickly negroes, who were liberated from the situation before described. If they appeared to be that kind of valetudinarians who were incapable of relieving their fellow sufferers. But to return to the sufferers when the delirium was banished by the re-assumption of the operations of nature. A scene ensued that seemed to deny that there was a perfect supreme ruler and unerring governor of the universe. Behold three hundred men, women and children, who, twelve hours before, enjoyed the purest freedom that nature herself could bequeathed to her natural offspring, who were untainted by vice, save only that corruption which those people had introduced among them--during the foregoing scene, the ship's crew weighed anchor, leaving this hospitable village without regret almost desolated. In a few days we came to a city, called in my language Guingana, where there was an English gentleman, who had resided there many months trading with the natives, during which residence he had courted and married the princess, only daughter and heir. He understanding, that an European vessel was going out, attempted to prevail upon his wife's father to consent that she might accompany him to his native country, but all entreaties were vain, until he interceded with the Judges whom he made believe that he would positively return with her in two years, and in the meantime give her an English education. The Judges interceded for him, and ultimately caused the prince to consent. On a solemn treaty being formed that he would take many ladies of honor to accompany her; with some young lads that were near allied to the throne; that he would give them all an European education, instruct them in all the arts of civilization in his power, and return in two years. For the true performance of this he pledged himself to the King and Judges in the most solemn manner.

Accordingly they all came on board the ship, accompanied with many of the nobility. The most solemn scene ensued that I ever beheld: offering up sacrifices, burning incense, washing and anointing their feet, and the consecrating their heir apparent of the throne, to the God of the Ocean, and to the protection of their great Father. The solemn dirge and the farewell sound of the trumpet, added sublimity as well as solemnity to the scene.

At the close of this ceremony were introduced abundance of rich presents for the outset and expense of the voyage, such as gold-dust, ivory, corn, rice with many other very valuable articles, which loaded the ship as deep as she would swim. The bride was decorated in the style of an eastern princess, with gold bracelets, rings, beads, and in fact was completely decorated in gold from head to foot.

As soon as we had fairly got under way, and about bidding adieu to the African coast forever, the captain and many of the officers made choice of such of the young women as they chose to sleep with them in their Hammocks, whom they liberated from chains and introduced into their several apartments. After the officers had provided themselves with mistresses of color, they made arrangements for the keeping and feeding the slaves. We were fastened in rows, as before observed, so that we could set upon our ramps or lie upon our backs, as was most convenient, and as our exercises were not much, we, it was concluded, could do with little food; our allowance was put at two scanty meals per day, which consisted of about six ounces of boiled rice and Indian corn each meal, with the addition of about one gill of fresh water; while in this situation, the ship's crew had been butchering a goat, and threw some meat, which fell near me, but a boy caught too quick for me, and swallowed it as soon as a hound would have done. I thought it was my right as it fell before me, and therefore clenched him, but one of my comrades interfered and admonishing us, said, it was extremely wrong for us to contend, as we had no parents or friends to take our parts, and could only bring disgrace upon ourselves. We desisted and mutually exchanged forgiveness.

Soon after this we were almost famished for want of water. We often begged salt water of the invalid who attended us. I would get it in my cap and cautiously drink it, which would run through us like salts. We were in such a situation that the officers liberated us, and Guy, the boy before mentioned, was so indecent as to drop some, from necessity upon the white man's deck. It was laid to another boy, who would not expose his friend, therefore he was saluted with only forty lashes, but poor Guy died a few days afterwards, and was thrown into the sea, which made food for sharks, as they continually followed us being well baited by the frequent deaths on board.

About this time the princess was delivered of a child, but the great disposer of all events, was pleased to waft its infant soul to realms unknown to us. There was great mourning among the maids of honor; they cried aloud.

A boy, one of my comrade slaves, by the name of Leo, forgetting his sufferings for a moment, was disposed to mirth; he observed, "Cordier agong, cadwema arroho:"-- which in English is, Hark! there is a trumpeter among us.

In this situation, upon the boisterous deep, where each gale wafted us to a return-less distance, from our families and friends, almost famished with hunger and thirst, to add horror to the scene, the sailors who were not provided with mistresses, would force the women before the eyes of their husbands. A sailor one day, forced the wife of a slave, by the name of Blay, before his face. Blay, whose blood boiled with wrath and indignation, said to his comrades in chains, Let us rise and take them, and force them to conduct us back to our native country again; there is more of us than of them, and who is there among us, who had not rather die honorably, than live ignominious slaves? The interpreter happened to overhear him, and gave information against him. Poor Blay was taken to the gunwale, and received 80 lashes, and was then put in chains, with a double weight of iron. At this treatment well may we cry out with Ezekiel-- "Behold their abomination in the sight of the Lord," After a voyage of about five months, the vessel arrived at Barbadoes, in the West-Indies, in the year of our Lord, one thousand seven hundred and fifty nine, or one thousand seven hundred and sixty, with the slaves, who had not either died with disease, mourned themselves to death or starved; many of the children actually died with hunger, pent up in the same ship where midnight and beastly intoxication, bloated the miserable owner. The cries of the innocent African boy, destitute of the protection of a parent, if they reached the ears, could not penetrate the heart of a Christian, so as to cause him to bestow a morsel of bread upon his infant captive, even enough to save his life.

The slaves, consisting of about three hundred in number, including women and children, were carefully taken out of the ship and put into a large prison, or rather house of subjection. In this house we were all, above twelve years of age, chained together, and sat in large circles round the room, and put to picking oakum. A slave by the name of Syneyo, from the town of Yellow-Bonga, taken in the manner formerly described, and who was one of the Judges in that place, refused to work. He rose up, and in his native language, made the following speech to the captain, which was repeated to him by the interpreter:

"Sir, we will sooner suffer death than submit to such abominable degradation. The brow of our great father, the sun, frowns with indignation on beholding the majesty of human nature abused, as we are, and rendered more brutal than the ravenous wild beasts, as ye are. Feel like mortal man, and what I say may prevent your spirit from being blotted out forever. You came to our country; you and your friends were treated with hospitality; we washed and anointed your feet; we gave you the best of our wines to drink, our most delicious food to eat; we entertained you with every amusement our country could afford. We prayed for you, burnt incense and offered up sacrifices for you; we gave you presents of gold, Ivory, corn and rice, with many other valuable things; and what return did you make us? You invited us to see your ship, we were credulous, even vigilance was asleep; you traitorously gave us opiates, which caused us to sleep, you bound us captives and bore us away to this place; you and your myrmidons ravished our wives and daughters, whipped us with many stripes, starved our children to death, and suffered others to die unnoticed. And now you hold us in bondage and oblige us to work unceasingly. Is this the reward of friendship, hospitality and protection? Are you a Christian people? Then do unto us as we have done unto you; strip us of these chains, and conduct us back to our own shores. If Christianity will not move you to perform so just an act, look at those little fatherless children, whom you kidnapped from their parents;--hear their cries, behold their sufferings, think of the bewailing of their bereft parents, look across the great waters to that village where you was almost idolized--view the distresses your conduct has brought upon it, & if you have one spark of human sensibility, or even the least shade of humanity, if you are what you profess to be, a Christian; repent and let us, whom you call heathens, return to our once happy shores, thereby, if you cannot obliterate, heal as much as possible the wounds you have made."

On the close of this speech, all was silent for a few minutes; but the captain in his turn made a speech more to the purpose. With a countenance, that would terrify a crocodile and a voice like the braying of a Jack-ass--he said:

"Oh you impudent, rebellious, treasonable, cowardly, saucy, low, black slave, I will teach you discipline, obedience, and submission, and what is more, I will learn you your duty. You seem to speak as though you thought yourself equal to white people, you Ethiopian black brute, you shall have but twelve kernels of corn per day----your breakfast shall be fifty stripes--and if your work is not done, I leave you to the care of this my overseer, who will deal with you as you deserve."

This order was strictly complied with. From Monday until Wednesday following, no one received any other allowance, except water, which we were driven to, in drove, and obliged to lie down and drink.

From Wednesday until Saturday, we had each, one ounce of biscuit in addition. All began to be subdued and to work according to their strength and abilities.

CONTENTS OF CHAPTER. 5.

CHAPTER. 5.

On Saturday morning, as I sat next to a girl by the name of Gow, who was a gentleman's daughter, sent from Guingana to this country for education, she was also accompanied by a little brother, about six years of age, who was under her protection. They both had been decorated in a style, equal to their rank, in their native country. Thry, her little brother happened to be asleep, and we sat pensively working as fast as our enfeebled bodies, and want of knowledge would permit.--All of us had been stripped of our ornaments, in fact, everything of value was taken from us, and instead of gold rings, bracelets of gold beads, chains and jewels, we had an old piece of sail cloth tied round our waists. She had been crying and sobbing all night, she said to me: What do you think your father would say, if he could see you in your present situation, stripped of his Cap and all the ornaments he gave you to wear when you went a swimming in the Neboah; and now chained and obliged to work both day and night unceasingly, and be whipped by those awful creatures, if you do not do, what is almost impossible to do.--On which nature gave way (perhaps moved by sympathy,) I burst into a flood of tears,

I being almost starved for want of necessary sustenance, even carrion would have been delicious. My change of fortune, stared me full in the face. I thought of home; I thought of a father's tenderness and a mother's love, a crowd of horrors burst upon me--we both cried aloud, until a feast of grief eased our swollen hearts; thus satiated we ceased to weep. Thry, her little brother, in the time awoke, and beginning to cry, he said to his sister--Come Gow, do get me a piece of bread and some water, for I am almost starved and am so thirsty that I cannot live----Come Gow, why won't you get it for me; you used to get me everything I wanted. O Thry, said she, I hope you will not cry, come sit down as it is impossible for me to assist you; I could die with pleasure if you were with our parents again. I have nothing that I can give you to eat or drink, being almost starved myself, and here I am chained you see, and If I do not do more work than I am able to do, I must be whipped and I fear they will kill me.--They both burst into a flood of tears, which continued for some time. After their lamentation ceased, she spoke to me, saying, I should not feel so bad if the white people had not taken from me the bracelet of gold, which was on my right arm, as my grand-father, when my grandmother died, took it from her arm and gave it to me (on account of my bearing her name) as a token of remembrance and affection, which was always expressed; and now I have nothing in this foreign land to remember her by, it makes me feel as if it would break my heart; but what is worse than all, I fear, if they don't kill me, they will take away my little brother; and if they don't starve him, he will mourn himself to death. At this instant the driver came in with a long whip under his arm, and placed himself in the centre of the circle in which we were chained, he stood about four minutes, cast his eyes upon the

71

slaves, a dead silence prevailed through the whole house except the re-echoing of sobs and sighs. He fixed his eye upon us, stepped up to the bunch of oakum which Gow had been picking, took it up in his hand with some vehemence, threw it down instantly, struck her upon the side of her head with the butt end of his whip, which laid her quivering upon the ground for one or two minutes. When she began to recover and to get upon her hands and feet, during which time he continued whipping her. Her little brother began to scream and cry, begging in his artless manner and unintelligible dialect for her relief. She at length regained her former situation, when he again turned the butt of his whip and struck her on the other temple, which leveled her with the ground; she seemed frantic, and instantly rose upon her feet, the driver with a terrible grin and countenance, that bespoke his brutality, struck her with a drawing blow over the left shoulder, which came round under her right arm, near the pit of her stomach, and cut a hole through, out of which the blood gushed every breath. The wretch continued whipping until he had satiated his unprovoked vengeance, then he sat her up and handed her a rope to pick, he composedly walked round to see some of the rest of the slaves. She sat reeling backwards and forwards for about two or three minutes, the blood gushing from her wounds every breath, then fell down and expired. There her little brother, went and laid his head upon her neck and said, Come Gow, don't cry any more, come get up, don't go to sleep and leave me awake, because I am so lonesome I cannot bear it, do wake up; O! I wish my father and mother would come and give us some water, for I must choke to death with thirst, if I cannot get some. He cried over her corpse some time and then went to sleep upon the dead body of his sister and protector, who was thus whipped to death innocent as our mother Eve in her primitive state when first she was placed in the garden of Eden.

During this time the humane Christian walked composedly up to me, and with a large tarred rope gave me about fifty stripes, which cut wails in every part of my body. At length I fainted, and when I recovered, this clement Christian white man had left this house of misery, and its inhabitants to ruminate upon their situation and the prospect before them.

We remained in this mansion dedicated to the subjugation of our spirits, for a few days, during which time many of my bosom friends were sold, and sent away and I unable to learn their destiny. At length a most affecting scene ensued. Mahoo, a nobleman's daughter, who was also sent from Yellow Bonga to this country for education, accompanied by her brother two years younger by the name of Bangoo; they had pledged themselves never to part but by death, let whatsoever fate await them, they were to lose their lives for each other, rather than be separated. But alas! Bangoo was sold and called for by the humane Christian purchaser, who had doubtless been devoted to the covenants of our Lord and Savior, perhaps had crossed himself before the image of Christ, suspended upon the cross. These poor creatures clung together, and by signs the most impressive that the pure aborigines of Africa could make, entreated the owner to suffer them to remain with each other. But they forced him away, tied him to a cart and drove it off, dragging him after it. She clung to him until a ruffian ran up, and with the butt end of his whip, struck her such a blow that she fell motionless upon the ground. She lay senseless for some time. As soon as she recovered, she was taken back to prison and here whipped forty lashes for her offence, or for the terror of others in like case offending. The poor creature was so maimed, that her life hung in doubt for three weeks. Thus were separated forever these two African children, neither purchased or stolen from their native land, but entrusted with many rich presents of bars of solid gold and ivory, to an enlightened, scientific, Christian people, who enjoy the light of divine revelation, and sent to this country, for the sole purpose of receiving a refined education.

Courteous reader, if you live in civilized society, and enjoy the privileges of an enlightened people; under the immediate light of gospel inspiration; or if you are only a moralist, and believe that man can be virtuous, without the restrictive influence of supernatural operation, ponder well upon these things. Proverbs, chap. 14, ver. 84.--Righteousness exalteth a nation; but sin is a reproach to any people.--We read again in sacred writ--Gen. chap. 9, ver. 6.--Who so sheddeth man's blood, by man shall his blood be shed, for in the image of God, made he man.--But what does the conduct of our advocates for slavery say to this doctrine or divine decree.--"Not so, my Lord, you did not mean that the African negroes should be included in this, thy Law, because they bear a different complexion from us thy chosen people. You only meant your law should extend to us to whom the regions of the north have given a light complexion, and who have the knowledge of thy laws. The poor negroes although they may have descended from the patriarch Jethro, the priest of Midian, who was one of the elders of thy chosen people, shall be cast off from the benefits of thy law and promises of the gospel. Therefore

74

we think the blood of this people will not be required at our hands. We can whip, scourge, torture and put them to death with impunity."

During our confinement in this prison the common sailors were allowed to come into the house and ravish the women in presence of all the assembly. Fathers and mothers were eye witnesses to their daughter's being despoiled. Husbands beheld their wives in the hands of the beastly destroyers. Children bore testimony of the brutality practiced upon their mothers.--"Behold their abomination in the sight of the Lord." 2nd Ezekiel.

We formerly mentioned the princess, daughter of the King of Guingana, who had been married to an Englishman. He was a very rich planter and slave owner on this island. The reader will recollect her husband's engagements to her Father, the Judges' solicitations, their treaty, the white man's vows, the king's hospitality, his presents in gold, ivory, corn, wine and oil; the young nobility and maids of honor that came out with her--Then mark the sequel. She was taken to her husband's dwelling, stripped of her ornaments, which consisted of immense sums of gold, as also of her clothing, her maids of honor were served in the same way, and all sent to the prison among the common slaves. She, on entering the house of subjection, and beholding her doom before her, fell into a fit of delirium, which continued with little or no intermission for two days. When the vehemence of grief and despair subsided, she became by degrees, more calm and sensible; she, not being chained, went out of the house, laid herself down upon the sand, and sang mournfully, in her native language, the following song.

1. Ye happy maids beyond the ocean's wave,
Who live secure from all these dread alarms,
Take heed from me, now dire affliction's slave,
Despise the beauties of the white man's charms.

2. Among my friends I play'd with every grace,
My hopes my prospects and my heart was free,
Amid this scene I view'd the white man's face, He lur'd me
trembling o'er the foaming sea.

3. With voice of Syren cloath'd with subtle guile,
He told the beauties of his native shore;
All these he said should court my placid smile,
All that my taste could wish or heart implore.

4. For him I left my home my mother's side,
For him I cross'd this boundless raging wave;

And now secur'd he spurns with haughty pride,
I'm lash'd and tortur'd, wretched, I'm a slave.

5. No friend endearing, wipes the falling tear,
No tender mother bends her pitying eye;
Far, far from home, no hopes my heart to cheer,
And none but monsters hear my dying sigh.

The driver whipped her back, tied her up and gave her eighty lashes, and set her picking oakum. Her tender fingers gave way and she could not sever the tarred cable. Her whipping had cut the flesh from her shoulder blades, so that the bone lay bare--her whole body was covered with wounds and wails of clotted blood. While in this situation her husband came in. As soon as her eye caught the image of her former adoration, and now author of her misery, she summoned all her strength and flew to his arms. But he, with a heart, harder than the adamantine rock, and colder than the mountains of lee in Greenland, calmly spurned her from him, with brutal insensibility. She stood motionless for some minutes, with a countenance expressive of the keenness of her afflictions. One moment ten thousand lightning's darted from her eyes, the next instant the mildness of the morning sun portrayed the tender emotions of her heaving bosom. Atlength she said:--

"Is it possible that the fair white man of the north, whose countenance is emblematical of the perfection of our great father the Sun, can thus spurn from his bosom, an innocent princess of the kingdom of Guingana, who forsook the splendor of her Father's Castle for his sake, and who but a few months ago enjoyed all the blessings of paternal affections in the sunshine of native innocence and prosperity? But lo! You came to our dominions, your beautiful appearance caused my Father to invite you to our castle, and suffer you to make it your home; the native splendor of our court was exhausted upon you every attention that was productive of your happiness, was paid to you by each member of the Court. I was ushered into your presence with all the splendor of African dignity! when you was weary, I strove to procure you rest, when thirsty, I gave you the best of our Wines to drink; I washed and anointed your feet, when you as an hungered I gave you the best of our fruits. When sick, I gave you Medicine and consolation. watched by day and night. You with every pretention of dignified love, with asseverations of the strongest, most pure and holy affection, solicited a union of our hands. At length you won my heart, and I consented to join our hands in the holy band of matrimony. Our Nuptials were celebrated, and we were both dedicated to the sun, according to the holy order of our religion.

Thus our matrimonial rites were consummated. I went into your arms with virgin purity, and the most unparalleled love. When you wished to leave our dominions--my father refused to let me leave his Court, as I was his only child and heir to his Throne. But you interceded with the Judges and Councilors, who prevailed upon my father to make a treaty, the conditions of which you well knew. You swore before the alter of incense burning, to give my suit an English education, to instruct us in all the arts of civilization, and return with us in two years. O thou polluter of our holy institution! what have you done? hear me and tremble. You have traitorously stole me from my country and friends; you, with the subtlety of the demon of seduction, with perjury and deception in your mouth, have destroyed me. You have made a father and mother miserable you have robbed me of all my precious jewels, and stripped me of my clothing, deprived me of liberty and even life itself, for I must soon die. See these wounds inflicted by your petty tyrants, see this tender flesh torn from my bones. Did you hate me? why all that assiduity? why not leave me with my father? Have you feelings? Look at this princely, tender, mangled frame, which you have so often embraced; see these wails inflicted by your order; upon whom? upon your wife, and mother of your deceased off-spring, whose soul looks down from Heaven, and sees your perfidy and my sufferings, and beholds me fast approaching him.--O Christian, wretch, traitor; I have done, I must die."

She swooned away, came to, raved and tore her hair in frantic ejaculations, and then expired. Luke, chap. 23, ver. 34--For if they do these things in a green tree, what shall be done in a dry.----James, iv--17--Therefore to him that knoweth to do good, and doeth it not, to him it is sin.--First Epistle of Peter, iv--18--And if the righteous scarcely be saved where shall the ungodly and sinner appear.

During all the foregoing scene, the planter stood apparently unmoved, but soon withdrew from the house, and I never saw him more. Thus we passed our time about two months, each day driven to water like beasts of the field, only we were chained together, and obliged to lie down in filthy brooks to drink, and the multitude would so roil the same, that the excrements from their necessary houses would be sucked in as we drank. In the meantime my ancles got sore in consequence of the chains; in short they were so galled that the driver thought if prudent to take off my irons, as maggots were making considerable inroads upon the sinews. Many of my companions were set at liberty on the same account. We stole out to beg for sustenance. The owners happened to be absent, and none but children were present. While a little girl was examining our appearance and listening to our unintelligible dialect, one of the boys who was taken with me went round into a back room, and got his cap full of stewed beans. He called us and informed us that he had got something that would make us feel better; we instantly left the house, went out and sat down in a circle under some shades, upon the bank of a muddy brook and soon licked them down to our great delight and benefit.

We had suffered for food in a manner and to a degree, of which even a faint description would be considered as fabulous, therefore I forbear to disclose it. Thus I remained for about three months from the time I was taken from the ship, starved, whipped and tortured in the most shameful manner, obliged to work unceasingly, in order I suppose that the element, benevolent and charitable Whiteman, should be satisfied that the heathen spirit, of an African boy of noble birth, should be sufficiently subdued, rendered tame docile and submissive; and all for my good that I should thereby become a tame, profitable and honest slave. The natural man must be obliterated, and degraded, that even the thought of liberty must never be suffered to contaminate itself in a negro's mind; and the odious thing, equality, should be taught by European discipline never to raise its head.

At length I was sold to Capt. Isaac Mills, who commanded a 44 gun frigate, and was led without much ceremony from the house of subjection to meet the man who thus owned me by right of purchase; which brings to my mind the following

SONG.

The Negro's Complaint.

By W. COWPER, Esq.

Forc'd from home and all its pleasures,
Afric's coast I left forlorn,
To increase a stranger's treasures,
O'er the raging billows borne.
Men, call'd christiains, bought & sold me,
Paid my price in paltry gold;
But though their's they have enroll'd me,
Minds are never to be sold.

Still in thought as free as ever,
What are Christian's rights, I ask,
Me from my delights to sever,
Me to torture, me to task?
Fleecy locks, and black complexion,
Cannot forfeit nature's claim;
Skins may differ, but affection
Dwells in black and white the same.

Why did all-creating nature
Make the plant for which we toil?
Sighs must fan it, tears must water,
Sweat of our's must dress the soil.
Think ye, masters, iron-hearted!
Lolling at your jovial boards,

81

Think, how many backs have smarted
For the sweets your cane affords!

Is there, as ye sometimes tell us,
Is there one who reigns on high?
Has he bid you buy and sell us,
Speaking from his throne, the sky?
Ask him, if your knotted scourges,
Fetters, blood-extorting screws,
Are the means which duty urges,
Agents of his will to use?

Hark! he answers--wild tornadoes
Strewing yonder sea with streaks,
Wasting towns, plantations, meadows,
Are the voice with which he speaks:
He, foreseeing what vexations
Afric's sons should undergo,
Fix'd their tyrant's habitations,
Where his whirlwinds answer--No.

By our blood in Afric wasted.
Ere our necks received the chain,
By the mis'ries which we tasted
Crossing, in your barks the main;
By our sufferings since ye bro't us
To the man-degrading mart,
All sustain'd with patience, taught us
Only by a broken heart.

82

Deem our nation brutes no longer,
Till some reason ye shall find
Worthier of regard, and stronger
Than the color of your kind.
Slaves of gold whose sordid dealings
Tarnish all your boasted powers,
Prove that you have human feelings
Ere you proudly question ours.

Here I would ask the reader and all mankind, whether a person or any other property, which is sold by any person, who has no other right, save that he immoral.

At any rate, I was conducted by two sailors, who led me as a beast to slaughter. I was so weak that I could not walk but a short distance, before I was obliged to rest, for I was so exhausted for want of food, that I was almost emaciated. And being forced from all of my comrades, and placed in a situation that I could not converse with any person, it forced upon me a fullness of grief that caused me to cry aloud, and then I expected my doom was certain death. The sand was hot and the journey fatiguing, yet it is now impossible for me to measure the distance in my own mind. At length we came to an Orange tree, where the oranges covered the ground; I would not ask for any, and dare not stoop down to pick any up, for fear of being whipped, although hunger that is indescribable, called aloud, urged, yes, almost forced me to partake of the forbidden fruit. We passed, and I was in an agony of despair; however, I was forced along to a house, which was inhabited by a man by the name of Welch, he had a black wife and white maid. The wife was as brutish and ostentatious as was Welch himself. She was a large fat greasy Guinea woman; flat nose, thick lips, with teeth as white as snow.—I was left in a stoop before the door. The captain who had bought me, and Welch, went into a room together, where they sat drinking and talking—perhaps this was his boarding house. While they sat regaling themselves with the inebriating drop, I remained in the stoop where I was first seated, imagining that they were planning my death.

While in this melancholy situation, as I sat musing upon my approaching fate, I discovered some Negroes and Mulattoes, boiling something in a large kettle. They seemed to be jabbering to each other. I fancied they were talking about me, and concluded that I was to be boiled in the same kettle. The thoughts of this horrid death, destroyed my hunger; every feeling except the thoughts of death, my native country and friends, sunk before the horror that pressed upon me. While I was thus situated, the white woman asked me into the house, or rather by signs, she induced me to go in. She let me set down and put into my hands one spoonful of pork and onions, which appeared had been stewed together. Also, a small piece of biscuit, which I ate without much indignation. It being about dusk, Welch came in and conducted me to a small back room, where the floor was sanded, and locked me in; there was neither bed nor chair in the room, therefore, I laid me down upon the floor and went to sleep, but I soon awoke and found I was extremely sick. I tried to get out, but found my efforts were vain. Accordingly I was obliged to puke upon the floor, after which I felt extremely weak and thirsty, but laid me down again upon the floor, and slept until sunrise. When I awoke, I heard some person at the door unlocking it. It was Welch himself, he opened the door, looked in and saw what I had done, returned, got a large whip, and the first salutation, after jabbering a few words, and frothing at the mouth, which was unintelligible to me, only I saw he was angry, he turned the butt of his whip, and knocked me down flat upon the floor. I, half stunned, attempted to get up, but he caught hold of my shirt, drew it over my head, and while he continued whipping; almost suffocated me. At length he tore off my shirt, which left me entirely naked as I was born; he again knocked me down, and continued whipping me. At this time the white woman came to the door, they had some words; I believe she undertook to expostulate with him, for he shook his whip at her, and she retired, then he resumed his whipping, until I fainted. After I was brought too, by the white woman, I found I was much bruised, and had bled much; and I could never, to this day discover but the blood had every appearance and quality of white man's blood. It was after 12 o'clock at noon, that I had any knowledge of anything which transpired after I fainted. Thus I was sold, and thus was I whipped, without being able to expostulate or enquire of my tyrant the reason for treating me in the foregoing manner; which forces upon me the following description of

THE NEGRO BOY.

The African Prince who lately arrived in England,
being asked what he had given for his watch, replied,
"What I'll never give again.--I gave a fine boy for it."

When avarice enslaves the mind,
And selfish views alone bear sway:
Man turns a savage to his kind,
And blood and rapine mark his way.
Alas, for this poor simple toy,
I sold a blooming Negro Boy.

His father's hope his mother's pride,
Tho' black, yet comely to their view:
I tore him helpless from their side,
And gave him to a ruffian crew;
To fiends that Afric's coast annoy,
I sold the blooming Negro Boy.

From country, friends and parents torn,
His tender limbs in chains confin'd,

I saw him o'er the billows borne,
And mark'd his agony of mind:
But still to gain this simple toy,
I gave away the Negro Boy.

In isles that deck the western wave,
I doom'd the hopeless youth to dwell:
A poor folorn insulted slave,
A beast that Christians buy and sell:
And in their cruel task employ,
The much enduring Negro boy.

His wretched parents long shall mourn;
Shall long explore the distant main,
In hopes to see the youth return;
But all their hopes and sighs are vain:
They never shall the sight enjoy,
Of their lamented Negro Boy.

Beneath a tyrants harsh command,
He wears away his youthful prime
Far distant from his native land
A stranger in a foreign clime:
No pleasing thoughts his mind employ,
A poor dejected Negro Boy.

But he who walks upon the wind,
Whose voice in thunder's heard on high,
Who doth the raging tempest bind,
Or wing the light'ning thro' the sky,
In his own time will soon destroy
Th' oppressors of the Negro Boy.

CONTENTS OF CHAPTER. 6.

CHAPTER. 6.

When I was fairly awakened, or rather brought back to my natural senses, I made shift to crawl out upon the stoop, where I sat down upon the bench and wept. While I was thus weeping there came along a black woman who discovered my tears, she asked me in the Bow-woo language, what I was weeping for although cheered, I was confounded. I felt as though it was a delusion. I said nothing; caution taught me there was deception. She then asked me what I wanted, when I ventured to speak, and tremulously told her, that I wanted nothing, for I dare not give any other answer. She then asked me where I came from--I told her ingenuously, that I came from the kingdom of Bow-woo. "What part of Bow-woo?" said she. I answered, The city of Deauyah and county of Hughlough. Hughlough, she exclaimed, What was your father's name? Whryn Brinch, says I, "And your mother's name was Whryn Dooden Wrogan--I knew her well----and can you remember your grand-father and mother?" O yes, said I. "What was your grand-mother's name?" Zoah. "How many children had she?" Three. "Do you remember Vossea?" O yes, I know them all. "Who preached in your church when you left home?" Caushee was our minister. "Caushee," she exclaimed, "is my mother's brother; if you know Gow Friendall's wife, you know my sister." That I do, and I well know Beanreau her son, for he was taken with me when we

88

went to swim in the Niger "O great father the sun, she exclaimed, has friend Whryn Dooden Wrogan a son in bondage, whom she will never more behold? And alas, has my dear sister Friendall lost forever her only son, to linger out a miserable existence in this foreign land. He, poor boy, was a playfull child, about four years of age, when I was taken. Do tell me where he is?" I told her he was sold some days before, and gone, I could not tell where. She wept for a few minutes, and then asked me to go into the house, and said she was sure I was hungry; I said no, I was not hungry, and that I did not wish to go in, as I was afraid of the white man. She told me the white woman was my friend, and would take care of me; and that she had two little girls, and I might have one of them to make me a wife to take care of me. I told her I did not want a wife, as I expected the white people would whip me to death, and I wished to die so that I could go back to my father and tell him what kind of beings there is in this country.

They then took me up and carried me to the house, told me I must eat something or I should starve. They gave me an earthen pitcher that had something in it like chocolate, and I drank it. They also gave me some bread and butter, but I could not eat it, as it looked so much like the pork that made me sick the night before. Then they gave me some crackers and I eat them. After I had eaten, she asked me a few questions and requested me to lie down, which I did. She told me she would stay by me and watch to see that no one offered to hurt me, but I must observe when her husband came, who was a white man, not to speak to her in my native tongue; neither would she speak to me, as it would displease him I was anxious to learn her story, and, at my request, she related it to me as follows:--

"When I was about seventeen years of age, I went down from Bow-woo to Bear-blea, the next province towards the sea. I remained there about three weeks on a visit, at my uncle's, Vroo Friend-all. I being decorated in a style different from their nation, I received much attention from the young gentry of the town, the name of which was Ghana. This town is situated on a small river, called Zoo, and falls into the Niger about nine miles below the town. A party of us one day went down to see the Niger, and amuse ourselves with such delights as might be met with. We stood upon an high bank of the river, when we discovered a boat containing white people. We anticipated their object as many people had been taken before. We flew, we separated, but a young man, whom I had become attached to, said he would not leave me, let the consequence be what it would. We hid ourselves in a thicket until night, then cautiously leaving our retreat, travelled towards the town. We had got within about two miles of home, thinking ourselves out of danger, began to talk, when in an instant we found ourselves surrounded. To contend was in vain to fly was impossible. We were without opposition bound and gagged, conducted to their boat which lay in the Zoo, not more than thirty rods from where we were taken. They had many there, and continued upon the search until morning, when they dropped down into the Niger, went down to the ship, which was anchored about thirty miles below the town; this was a French vessel. In short, we came to Martinico, where we were landed and sold at auction. Vrocea, for that was my friends name, was taken from me, I was sold to a French merchant, and put into his kitchen.

Vrocea found means to meet me afterwards, as he lived about two miles from town and came there often. Our affections increased, we contrived our escape. An English vessel lay at anchor in the harbor, the captain was frequently dining with my master. I found an opportunity to let him know my wishes, he promised me liberty and protection if I would go with him. Accordingly Vrocea and myself were conveyed on board the night before he was to sail. We met with nothing until we had been out about three days, when we were attacked by a Spanish vessel. They were beaten off although of far superior force; but alas! My beloved Vrocea bravely fell in the contest. Thus all my hopes of happiness were obliterated forever.

"We made a long voyage, and at length arrived at this island. I lived in the captain's house for about two years. He dressed me elegantly, treated me tenderly, seated me at the head of his table at all times; and as I then spoke French, I soon learned English. At length he offered me his hand. It was bettering my situation, therefore I accepted his offer. We were married about seven years ago, and have two little girls and a boy. My husband's name is Lecois, he has left the seas, & owns a small plantation; he is a man of pleasure and considerably dissipated; he is a natural tyrant, but has much feeling and uses me well, only sometimes when intoxicated."

I listened to the foregoing account with delight, and notwithstanding my situation, I was overjoyed, to see a distant relative, and one that came from my native place; but even that joy gave me pain. I lay musing for some time, burst into tears and cried myself to sleep. When I awoke, it was almost sun-down. The black woman was gone. I felt worse than ever, as I had no one to speak to, and thirst suffocated me almost to death, and I was so sore, I could not rise up alone. The white woman helped me up, and led me to the stoop. While I sat there crying, a little Mulatto girl came and said something to me, and gave me a piece of ginger bread. This girl, I suppose, was daughter to my friendly country woman; but I could not understand what she said, neither could I eat one atom of the bread, in consequence of my being so overcome with thirst. At this time an old black man came along, and said to me, "are you here today boy." I said yes, how do you do today? says he, O I am almost dead, for I want to see some friends, and I am whipped almost to death; then I asked him if he had been to the slave prison today? he said he had, and that they were all well. Ah! said I, I wish I was along with the boys again. He tried to cheer me up, told me they would use me better by and by. I saw he had a barrell on a dray, I asked him what he had in his barrell? he said, nothing, but water, and that is old sea water, which is all rotten' with maggots; I begged most earnestly, as I was almost dying with thirst, he got an old dish and brought me some, The slime and maggots almost thickened it, yet I drank, straining it as much as possible through my teeth. The most delicious wine, slaking the thurst of the most refined Prince on earth, was never more grateful to the taste, than this water was to me. Neither was the good Samaritan better employed than was my humane African friend. When I reflect upon the wants, miseries, and dependencies of mankind, I cannot conceive of a more humane act than was thus performed by a Slave.

After I had thus been relieved from the torments of thirst, I eat the gingerbread, but could not eat the biscuit and butter, before mentioned. It being dusk, Welch came, took me by the shoulder and put me into the back hole, and again locked me in. In this solitude I met the most horrid nightly visions that the human mind can experience. Whether I slept or was awake, I am unable to say, at any rate, I thought, Maggots were devouring my inwards and whips were scourging my back; the furies of unprovoked vengeance were preying upon me to that degree that I was almost tempted to wish for annihilation. In the morning, I was unable to rise, I found myself in a violent fever, and lay three weeks in a most hopeless and abandoned situation, nothing but the arm of Almighty Jehovah saved my life.

But to give Justice where Justice is due, the white woman paid every attention in her power, when Welch was gone; and my country woman paid every attention in her power,--but Welch's wife never entered the room during my sickness.

As soon as I was able to walk, Capt. Mills called for me to go on board of his frigate. He brought me a sailors Jacket and Kilts, and a new white Shirt.

While I was putting them on in his cabin, he rubbed his hand across my back, then clapped them together, signified to me that I had been whipped, and made signs that he wished to learn the author. He called me upon deck, I pointed to the place, which was in sight, and by signs, as intelligible as possible for me, informed him, who had thus whipped me.

He expressed to me by signs, the strongest indignation, and I believe would have revenged himself upon Welch, if he could have met him, but he was under sailing orders, and immediately put to sea, as I afterwards learned that he belonged to admiral Hawk's fleet, which was then under sailing orders, upon a private expedition, against St. Croix; I also learned he had seen me in the house of Subjection, and purchased me for his cabin boy, or private waiter. But I being unable to understand the language, did not answer his wishes; therefore I was put among the mariners and taught the military discipline by one William Burks, who taught me altogether by signs. When we arrived at St. Croix, we received orders to sail for St. Augustine, where we tarried only two days, then sailed for the Havannah, or, as it was called new Spain, on the grand expedition to reduce that place.

On our passage we lost sight of the guide ship, just before day, in consequence of a thick fog, we got wind bound and could not find the fleet. While thus stranded, a Spanish 64 came up to us, and ordered us to strike. Capt. Mills told him, that he would never strike to any Spanish or French force, until he had given his English tars an opportunity to try their bravery, and demanded in turn their surrender. Our ship was prepared, and every man upon his post.

Here it is my duty to acknowledge, that I saw heroism clothed in submission; bravery docile; the spirit of man commanded still independently brave, one gave a pledge of his fair mistress to his friend, with solemn injunctions; another a commission to his wife and children, and another to his parents. Their only fear seemed to be that their friends could not learn that they died bravely fighting for their king and country, In short, the memory of their actions seemed to be their glory. The Spanish ship bore down upon us; the captain had given orders to take the first broad side and tack, so as to get the wind, and be prepared for the second fire, also that our smoke might assist us and injure them. Strict orders were given, that there should not be a gun fired. I not understanding their language, when we first received their broadside, thought it my duty to answer it, therefore took up my gun and fired upon them. When they came opposite to us on the second tack, we immediately gave them a broadside.

The battle lasted about fourteen minutes, and at the expiration of which time they immediately struck, and yielded themselves up to us as a lawfull prize.

CONTENTS OF CHAPTER. 7.

CHAPTER. 7.

But during this battle, I can observe, that I felt no other sensation than that if they killed me, I should go to my great father the sun; therefore I courted death.

I stood upon the upper deck, exposed to all the enemies shot for about seven minutes, contemplating a meeting with my grand-father, who had gone before me. I was disappointed, for I received five wounds, and was conveyed to the surgeon's apartment; on examination of which three were upon my head very slight, one on my ankle, where a musket ball passed through; the fifth was caused by a musket ball entering by the side of my back bone and lodging in my right hip. The surgeon tried to extricate the ball, but I not understanding the object shouted like a Loon, and would not permit him to probe the wound.

In consequence of my firing without orders, instead of punishment with death, as would have been the fate of one doing the same, understandingly, the captain gave me the honorable nick-name of Jeffrey. I say honorable, as I was named after Sir Jeffrey Amherst, General and commander in chief of the expedition for the reduction of Canada, the year before. The reader will recollect the taking of Quebec, in consequence of the memorable battle upon the plains of

Abraham, before the city, fought by young General Wolfe, commander of the British army, and General Montcalm, who commanded the French in which the former was victorious, and caused the place to surrender to the arms of the English.--Many have the mistaken idea that Wolfe was commander in chief; but the fact is, Amherst bore the chief command. And his character was, that he was one of the bravest men in the realm of Great Britain; but he possessed rather more courage than prudence. As my act of firing bore some resemblance of courage and want of prudence, and Jeffery being a suitable name for a negro boy, I was dubbed with it at that time, and have ever borne it since, only they have lately added nick-name upon nick-name, for people call me old Jeff now. But to return--I was confined with my wounds for about two months, in which time we sailed to Savannah, in the state of Georgia, with the prize. We stayed in this place but few days, in order to make some repairs and take in fresh water; then we sailed to join the fleet. After we joined it, we were informed that the French and Spanish fleet had joined, and that they were about to attack Gibraltar. Admiral Hawk gave orders for the fleet to stand for that place, but when we arrived we found we had been misinformed, therefore we sailed for the Havannah. While on the passage, Capt. John Staley, a brave commander of an English frigate, got becalmed and lost sight of the fleet. While in this situation he was attacked by a Spanish ship of superior force. They fought about two hours and forty minutes. Staley having expended all his ammunition except one round, hoisted a flagg of truce and informed the commander of the Spanish ship that he had two hours to determine whether he would surrender himself and force honorable prisoners of war, or be sunk; for if he had to spend any more lives, he would give nor take quarters. After a short consultation the Spaniards surrendered on certain honorable conditions. He conducted his prize to the fleet, and there was great rejoicing when he joined us. But when the Spanish captain learned the situation of the frigate when he surrendered, he was extremely mortified, and discovered some signs of insanity.

We at length arrived before the fortress at the Havannah, where we remained about two months. When all the English forces were collected, we commenced the attack in the following manner:--

We landed between four and five thousand troops, to make an attack by land. The Spanish made a sally from the fort, placed their cavalry in front, who commenced the attack on their part. They were met by a regiment of Scotch highlanders, who fought with broad swords, and with great dexterity cut one rein of their horseman's bridles, which turned them round upon their foot and created great confusion and prodigious slaughter, which decided the battle. In the meantime the fleet kept up a continual firing upon the town and fort. I saw the steeple of their principal church shot down, and many public buildings. The form of the attack by the shipping was singular, and one of the most sublime sights ever seen by man. Figure to yourself thirty two seventy four gunships of the line, and six frigates, passing in a circle as near to each other as possible, and when they came opposite the fort, they gave a broadside, which kept up a continual thundering of cannon for eighteen hours, which made a breach in the walls. The Spanish sent a flag of truce and surrendered unconditionally to our forces. After which the whole island fell into the hands of the English. After this victory we sailed to Dublin, the capital of Ireland. This was the first time I ever saw a capital European city. We remained here about three weeks. then we sailed for Savannah, in Georgia, leaving the fleet behind. Here I was, by the kindness of captain Mills, allowed many privileges; and to do Justice to his name, I must here observe, that he was a brave and humane man. He was never rifled with passion, and in battle as unmoved as mount Atlas. The whole ship's crew loved, respected, and revered him. He took great pains to learn me English, in which by this time I had made some progression. We spent about four weeks at Savannah, then we sailed for New York, where we staid about ten days, from thence we sailed to Newport, R. Island, here we made but a short stay and then sailed for Halifax; on our passage we caught many codfish, and I was sat to cleaning them, in doing which I cut my hand, and while it was bleeding one Pattle, who was bantering with my master for me, came and took hold of my nose and chin, opened my mouth as a jockey would a horse's, in order to see my age or to insult me. While my mouth was open, he spit a cud of tobacco into it which made me sick, I sat down and wept all day, and since which I could never chew that weed.

From Halifax we sailed to Boston, where we tarried about two months, where I was again indulged by my master, who allowed me to go about the town. I became acquainted with many free African descendants, who appeared to be well contented in their situation. They asked me many questions about my native country. I gave them the best account in my power, which appeared to gratify them, and procure me much attention. I was extremely anxious to remain in this place, but was at length obliged by the authority that held me, to sail to New Haven,

Connecticut, where we arrived about the first of October. There was frost snow and ice upon the ground which was the first I had ever seen, the reader may well judge, it was a miracle to me.

Here I bid adieu to the British fleet forever, as I was sold to a man belonging to Old Milford, west side of Oyster river. His name was John Burrell, a professed puritan. The snow was about two inches deep, and I had on a thin linen jacket and one pair of trousers or sailor's kilts and no shoes. I was the first night put upon the naked hearth to sleep, but could not enjoy the sweets of repose, for a British man of war was a palace in comparison to my present situation, in which I had been upwards of two years. The next night I met the same fare, which was continued for about two weeks. My wounds, which I received from the Spaniards, broke out newly and I almost perished with cold and hunger, and as this puritan Christian could not condescend to give me anything to eat but old crusts and bones, such as people generally throw to their dogs, and nothing to sleep upon but a cold stove, not even a blanket or old quilt could be allowed. He would read the bible and pray both night and morning, for all mankind, recommend all to the sovereign mercy of the father of the universe; sit down to a good breakfast and when he had glutted himself he would throw down a bone upon the hearth before the block where I was allowed to sit, and sometimes it would be accompanied by a crust of bread, which would all perhaps make six ounces of coarse food. If it was sunday morning he would dress himself, put on his best coat and wig, go to meeting, there sit and appear to suck in every word the minister should say. He would also suffer me to stand behind the door of his sanctuary.

One night I dreamed of being in my native country, and conversing with one of my aunts, by the name of Zoah. In this vision a region of imaginary happiness appeared before me. I was in a complete transport of earthly felicity; but alas! a slave upon a cold stone in a foreign land; When I awoke I found it was a dream. I was also in extreme agitation and almost chilled to death, which freighted me so that I cried aloud. I rose up and put together some brands, attempting to make some fire to warm me. Something was said by my master. He spoke so quick that I did not understand him, then immediately jumped up, and the first salutation knocked me down with his fist. As I went to get up he took up a chair and struck me on the side of the head near where I had been wounded in the first battle I was engaged in, and pealed up a piece of my scalp about as big as my three fingers. I fell with the blow under a table, where he kicked and beat me until I became insensible. When I awoke in the morning I found myself in a most shocking situation. The blood had ran across the room and stood in a puddle in short, I was covered with wounds and poorly fitted for the service of the day; but work I must, as there was no charity to be found in my master's breast. I was ordered to go upstairs to get some corn, and while I was going to the pen to give it to the swine, there being a hole in the bottom of the basket, some of the ears dropped upon the ground. My puritan master gave me two or three strokes with his whip. When they handed me my bones to pick I could not eat, and they thought I was sulky. Burrell handed me the bone, took his horse-whip, and lashed me until I gnawed it like a dog. When this was over, I was ordered to go about a quarter of a mile barefoot to get some turnips, as I could not move fast, it seemed as if it would freeze my feet, The keenness of the pain caused me to make use of every exertion to keep the frost from nipping my toes. In the mean-time someone of the family had drawn some beer or cider, I went to drink some of it, my mistress saw me and knocked me down with the distiff and ordered me to go to chopping wood. I not being used to chopping, cut my foot, it bled much and I bound it up with some husks, then laid down between two logs. While I lay in this situation, one Mr. Samuel Eals came and took me up, and very charitably led me into the house, told Burrell that such abuse was inhuman and unchristian; he also threatened to complain of him to the authority. They quarreled for some time then he gave me his great-coat and sat me down by the fire, and went to one James Parker, got a pair of shoes and took me with him. Isaiah, 58 chap. 3, 4, 5, 6 and 7th verses----Amos, 5th verse 25th.--Often have I been caused to reflect upon the conduct of this man towards me, as he was one of the strongest professors in the church, and as strict in his family devotion as any man I was ever acquainted with; and he must have been a hypocrite, and never received that grace which worketh a change of heart, and drives out that evil which was ingrafted into man by the fall. If he had charity, that crown of Christian virtues, how could he pray for all mankind and then starve a poor negro boy, who could look to no other person for food. If he had a hope of grace and mercy from his Lord and Master, how could he freeze his slave, and then unmercifully beat him for attempting to make a fire to warm himself. Did he think me in possession of an immortal spirit? Then what could he make of the Lord's prayer----"Forgive us our trespass, as we forgive those that trespass against us." If I had done wrong how could he expect his sins to be forgiven him? In short, was there a single trait of a real and true christian in him? But the advocates of a distinction in human nature may say, I have no right to examine into the acts and feelings of white people to such I answer, If I have the same propensities and feelings, and endowed with the same intellectual reason, then where is the distinction? Is it the color or is it the power you have gained over me, which the once first angel in heaven, now the arch fiend of hell, attempted to gain over his creator? From what fountain does the Ethiopian, Turk, Indian, Chinese, Tartar or Englishman receive all their sensations. Is there more than one supernatural creating power; or is that power partial in the distribution of his spirit? No. The house of subjugation, the difference in education and situation, is all. Even in this country, where the African is degraded and disgraced; his heart broken, his hope destroyed, and almost generally deprived of education. Do you not see some geniuses burst forth and rise above the tyranny and oppression they are under, and stand as monuments of admiration. Behold some of your ministers of the gospel! Go to the African churches, in the cities of New York and Philadelphia, see their devout attachment to the religion of their Savior. Hear the pathetic and persuasive eloquence of their preachers, and then answer my inquiries.--But to the narrative.

At night Mr. Eals made me a straw bed, which was the first bed I had slept upon after I was taken into bondage, until this time. This humanity, and christian like act, opened my wounded feelings and brought my sorrows up a fresh to my view. My mother's tenderness came to my recollection, being so much subject to abuse, the least kindness brought upon me that kind of melancholly, which a real christian feels to see his brother devout in christian faith, depart this life. At night I dreamed that the good spirit came to me, took me by the hand, asked me to accompany him, which I did without the least hesitation. He ascended with me high above the earth, and wafted me through vast space--at length we arrived at the African coast and came in sight of the Niger, following its course up the river, about one hundred yards above the earth. He shewed me the desolated town of Yellow Bonga. The shades of night seemed to break away, and all at once he gave me a fair view of Deauyah, my native town. The people were all asleep, and we hovered about the town until it was light. We then descended and sat upon the grass before the church.

CONTENTS OF CHAPTER. 8.

CHAPTER. 8.

I then thought I had died of my wounds, and that our great father, the Sun, was the good spirit, who conducted me back to my town. The spirit left me, and seemed to ascend into the air with dazzling light, which overpowered the strength of my eyes to behold. I started at the sight and awoke. The fire from the kitchen hearth had blazed up and shone bright in my face--So I came from Africa without the help of any other spirit save only necessity, much quicker than I went, and found myself still a forlorn slave, as I went to sleep. Mr. Samuel Eals used me very well while I remained with him; but as soon as I was able to work, I was sold to one Peter Pridon, son of the old priest Pridon, of Old Milford. I lived with him about two months, and got five severe whippings for crying nights. From Pridon I was bartered away for some old horses to one Gibbs, who was a man of very inferior talents, possessing great pride and ostentation, always at work and in a hurry. He had the longest nose and chin I ever saw attached to a man's face, thin lips, and a voice that was less pleasing than the ravens. With this man I stayed about three months, and to describe the particular management of his family would only mortify those who live in the same way at the present time. I have thought he took a peculiar delight in whipping me, as I uniformly received about four whippings per day. If I was awkward, cried too much, or was lazy, it was sure to purchase me a good drubbing. Sometimes I got a flogging for freezing my feet while I was foddering and cutting the ice out of the watering place. And one day, while I was getting corn up stairs, I designedly pushed his boy down stairs, for while I had the basket upon my shoulder he began whipping me, & chirping to me, as would a driver to his horse. For this I was knocked down stairs, basket, corn and all shared the same fate; and to complete my punishment, the next morning I received fifty lashes with a horse-whip. Next I was sold to Phineas Baldwin, of the town of Old Milford. I continued with him until summer, or rather spring, when I went to live with his son Phineas, who had two small children to tend. In his nursery I was engaged until the last of May, when I was sold to Jones Green, of the same place. Green did not whip me but about twice in a week, except now and then a kicking. From Green I was transferred to one Murrier, a tanner, where I remained until September, at which time the widow Mary Stiles, of Woodbury, Connecticut, bought me. This was a glorious era in my life, as widow Stiles was one of the finest women in the world; she possessed every Christian virtue. This same woman was the mother of Benjamin Stiles, Esq. whose illustrious character is rewarded in the heart of every person living who knew him.

Here the prospects of the negro boy began to wear a more pleasing appearance. To mention all the incidents of my life during my residence in this family, for sixteen years, would make a volume; therefore I will only mention a few. This good lady learned me to read. One day I was sent to school, where I was taught to read by the master. I could not speak plain, therefore when I came to W I could not pronounce it and when I attempted so to do, I was understood to say devilyou. He thought I said so in order to insult him, and therefore was angry, and with his ferule struck me. The second time he struck me his ferule broke, and he ordered me to sit down; but I concluded I would not stay there to be whipped by a schoolmaster, therefore I walked out instead of sitting down. He called me back; but I had not the least idea of stopping, therefore composedly walked off. I expected he would follow me, and had determined in my own mind to give him a whipping, as I verily believed the task would be easy. Anger prompted me to this determination; but he did not follow me. Prudence kept him back, and vengeance melted me into pity, for I pitied his want of discernment and just judgment. Thus I became a child again; I went into the nursery and shed tears, where I sat about an hour. At length I went in and Mrs. Stiles asked me what they had done to me, and how I liked going to school. She was questioning me as her grandchildren had told her what happened. I felt some compunction, although not guilty of any intentional wrong. She questioned me for some time with all the humanity of a saint, then generously told me I should not be whipped at school, for she would learn me to read herself. Accordingly she with intentions as good and pure as virtue itself, taught me to read and speak the English language. She was indefatacable until I could read in the bible and expound the scriptures, in the meantime she taught me the prayer usually communicated to children, and some general principles of the Christian religion. Both day and night she most kindly taught me, by which I am enabled to enjoy the light of the gospel.

When this lady died I descended like real estate, in fee simple to her son Benjamin Stiles, Esq. About four years after her death, her two sons, Benjamin and David, were drafted to fight in the revolution. I also entered the banners of freedom. Alas! Poor African Slave, to liberate freemen, my tyrants. I had contemplated going to Barbadoes to avenge myself and my country, in which I justified myself by Sampson's prayer, when he prayed God to give him strength that he might avenge himself upon the Philistines, and God gave him the strength he prayed for.

I went into Capt. Granger's company, from hence I was drafted into Capt Borker's company of light infantry, as they wanted six feet men. I then wanted but a quarter of an inch of being 6 feet 3 inches. We marched to Frog Plain, from there to second hill, between Reading and Ridgold. On the Spring we came to Pauncludg there to Salem. General Worcester commanded the British under the command of general How, who attacked us. We beat them back; the fight was continued all day, and the victory was sometime doubtful.

From thence we marched to White-Plains, I devoted myself to study, making some philosophical observations on vegetation & c.

From White-plains, we marched to Fort Montgomery, at which place we remained until June. From thence we proceeded to Mud-Fort, where we encamped until August.

In the latter part of the month of August the Fort was attacked, and after every exertion we could possibly make, we were obliged to surrender to superior force; and we retreated to Kingsbridge. Soon after our arrival at

Kingbridge, New York was evacuated, and we entered the city under the command of Col. Owin, from Rhode Island.

However previous to the evacuation of New York, I was one of a hundred, selected for the purpose of plundering a certain British Store, which was completed without the loss of a single man--but with the gain of seven loads of excellent Provisions.

We were overtaken by the British, after we had marched about a mile towards North Castle. The party that perused us were 60 light dragoons, whom we soluted so warmly with a well-aimed fire: that they were obliged to return for additional force. They again overtook us about 3 miles from New York, but as we had also some new forces, they thought most proper to return without an engagement.

We then proceeded to North Castle, uninterrupted, where we continued about 2 months. From thence we marched to New-Windsor, where we spent the remainder of the season. From thence we marched to West Point, and took up winter quarters. While we remained here the soldiers played many boyish pranks. One Samuel Shaw, a brave soldier, but as complete a petty thief as ever graced a camp; not that I would represent him a thievish character; as honesty was never more predominant in any human being, than it was in him, when he pledged himself to any fellow soldier. However he with myself and some others from our camp, the day before we were to be reviewed, by his Excellency, Gen. George Washington, concluded we would have a soldier-like frolic. Accordingly we secretly stole from the lines, went to a Farm not many miles distant, which was occupied by a Tory. From him we stole a shoat.

Shaw was the principle manager in this affair, and we got into camp just before day. We laid the Shoat in the middle of the camp, and sat down, and in the language of gratitude, began conversing upon our success; but short was our confab. As we soon saw the frothing Tory coming for his Hog. We immediately covered ourselves with our blankets and effected to be asleep. He recognized his property; he went to the Col. to whose regiment we then belonged, and reported that we had stolen one of his shoats. Col. Melgs, came immediately to our company, and with a countenance, that plainly bespoke a determination of punishing us if guilty. He asked how we came by that Shoat; I answered immediately that the owner had brought it for sale, but that from his manner of conversation (knowing him to have been a tory) we unanimously suspected him to have come as a spy, and were determined to keep the Shoat until the officers might have an opportunity of being acquainted with his designs. My fellow soldiers were glad of the opportunity of confirming the truth of my assertion--which so completely satisfied the Col. of our innocence, together with the circumstance of its lying in fair view, in the middle of the Camp--that he severely reprimanded the man for his insult on him and his soldiers. The man a little frightened at so unexpected a charge of guilt that he really had the appearance of a condemned culprit, and was glad to escape with his dead pig upon his back.

A few days after this circumstance took place----Shaw with two others of which I was one, had been out on an expedition; in which we became extremely hungry. Shaw proposed to furnish meat if we would procure bread; all accordingly offered to do it. Shaw went to a Dutchman's house, not far distant and with artful affection of great fatigue and an ingenious representation of his sufferings excited the old ladies' compassion, to a great degree--and she offered him a bottle of rum--he took a good draught of rum and pretended to be greatly strangled, the woman pitying his situation, went to the well for water. Shaw improved that opportunity to put a large gammon that hung in the chimney-corner into his knapsack. The woman returned with some water, which soon relieved Shaw----he then asked for some bread and milk--while he was eating, he was also busy in putting Spoons into the legs of his stockings--After we had got some distance from the house, we asked Shaw what could tempt him to take so much from the seemingly good old woman, he said that he had long known the old Dutchman to aid and assist the British, or he could not have had a heart to do it, which account of the Dutchman we afterwards learned was correct. Nothing of consequence took place that related to me till spring, when we moved to Hackensack in the Jerseys. Soon after our arrival there, the enemy stole some cattle from our lines. Capt. Granger with twenty chosen men was sent in pursuit of them, with orders to go about two miles to a place called Hackensack-four-corners. I was one of the number, but when we arrived at the destined place, we discovered that they had passed with the cattle; one Ahiel Bradley, a sergeant in the company said if myself and one Adam Waggonor, would accompany him, he would go and find them, as he believed that they were driven to a certain meadow back from the road, which meadow he was acquainted with. The captain consented and we pursued our course upon the track, to a pasture fronting the meadow, into which we discovered they had been driven, we came to a small hill or rise of land over which they must have passed. This rise being covered with bushes, it was thought prudent, that I should wait upon the hither side of the hill while they went over and examined into the fact, whether the cattle were actually in the meadow or not, and at the same time, to keep a look out for the enemy. While I stood there anxiously waiting for their return, I suddenly discovered a man riding up to me not more than eight rods distant on full speed with a pistol in his hand, and ordered me to lay down my arms. But not being so instructed by my officers you may well suppose that I did not. At first I thought he was a Jerseyman and was attempting to fool me, as they had played some such pranks before, upon some of the soldiers belonging to our line--therefore in return I demanded to whom I was to surrender and by what authority he demanded it.--he said I must surrender to him who demanded me in the name of the King his majesty of Great Britain. I then plainly told him that neither him or his King's majesty would get my arms unless he took them by force. He immediately cocked his pistol and fired; I fell flat upon the ground in order to dodge his ball, and did so effectually do it, that he missed me. I rose, he drew his sword and rode up to me so quick that I had no time to take aim before he struck my gun barrel with his cutlass, and cut it almost one third off--also cut off the bone of my middle finger on my hand, as he struck the horse jumped before he could wheal upon me, again although' my gun barrel was cut, I fired and killed him, as he fell I caught his horse and sword. He was a British light horseman in disguise.--I mounted immediately, and that instant discovered four men on horse back approaching me from different direction, I fled, passed one man, just before I came to a stone wall. Both of our horses were upon the full run he fired and missed me. My horse leaped the wall like a deer; they all

112

pursued me. When we got into the road, they were joined by many more; and all with swords in hand pursued me in full career. I drove my horse as fast as possible, stabbed him with my sword and gun, kicked my heals in his side, but having no spurs, and not being so good a horseman they gained upon me. I looked forward and saw my Capt. in full view, almost a mile distant. This encouraged me, and the long shanked negro, soldier with a leather cap, mounted on an elegant English gelding light horse, made all whistle again. When I came in about twenty or thirty rods, I heard the Captain say, "there come one of our leather caps, and it is Jeffrey.--reserve your fire so as not to kill him; however the men fired, and three balls cut my garments, one struck my coat sleeve, the next hit my bayonet belt, and the third went through the back side of my leather-cap. They were so close upon me, that the same fire killed four of the British and five horses--and wounded some more; I did not stop for this salute, but pulled on for head quarters. When our men fired the enemy were within two or three jumps of me; but being so handsomely saluted upon surprise, as our men were concealed from their view, they made the best retreat possible.

CONTENTS OF CHAPTER. 9.

CHAPTER. 9.

I made no halt until I arrived within our Camp. When I dismounted tied my horse and went to set up my gun, I found I could not open my hand which was the first time that I discovered that I was wounded. As slight fear and precipitation had turned me almost as white as my fellow soldiers. In consequence of my wounds, I was unfit for duty again for almost three months. But after all the poor simple Negro was cheated out of his horse; as I sold horse saddle and bridle, holsters, pistols and sword, to col. R. Sherman for his contract of two hundred and fifty dollars, who thought proper never to pay the same. Yet I felt more gratitude towards the horse than regret for the loss of him, as he with the assistance of divine providence saved my life.

And here I will observe, that I can give no other reason why the enemy did not fire upon me, only I presume, they choose to take me alive, which they had full faith in, as they when our men fired upon them were fast approaching me--and what caused me to form this opinion, I had been one of the standing century upon the outposts for some time, therefore I presume they concluded that I would acquaint them with the state of our army. Perhaps the soldiers thought I might be sold by them and enrich their coffers; as these mercenary beings seem rather more inclined to deal in human flesh and blood than in fighting.

I belonged to one capt. Baker's company when the attack was made upon us at Hackensack, I was on the flank and the charge was made there; we gave them a warmer salute, and lost many brave Yankee-boys. Our Battalion was charged by their light horse, and we beat them off with our bayonets.

After this battle, we heard that the enemy were making their way to Stanford, we marched there immediately, and arrived before them. A party marched down into some meadows to watch their motion; on discovering their superior force, we fired upon them and ran off fully believing,

>"That he who fights and runs away,
>May live to fight another day--

We concealed ourselves behind a stone wall for some minutes, they lost sight of us, but continued firing for some time; as we were passing over a small rise of ground several balls whistled by us, and what was peculiarly diverting to us; one Calob Nicholas dodged a bullet after it had passed us for above 5 seconds. We ran to the fort at Stanford but the enemy had gotten possession; we then took again to our heels, we then retreated to Salem from thence we marched to West point, where we remained until September. From thence we went to Horseneck--where we remained until winter; frequently searching about the adjacent country. Finally I was in the battle at Cambridge, White plains, Monmouth, Princeton, Newark, Froggs-point,

Horseneck where I had a ball pass through my knapsack. All which battels the reader can obtain a more perfect account of in history, than I can give. At last we returned to West point and were discharged; as the war was over.-- Thus was I, a slave for five years fighting for liberty.--After we were disbanded, I returned to my old master at Woodbury, with whom I lived one year; my services in the American war, having emancipated me from further slavery, and from being bartered or sold.--My master consented that I might go where I pleased and seek my fortune. Hearing flattering accounts of the new state of Vermont; I left Woodbury, and travelled as far as the town of Lenox, in Massachusetts, where for the first time I made a bargain as a freeman for labor; I let myself to a Mr. Elisha Orsborn for one month, at the price of five dollars. When I had fulfilled this contract, I travelled to the town of Poltney in Vermont, there again I let myself to a Mr. Abiel Parker, for the sum of thirteen pounds ten shillings, for six months. Here I enjoyed the pleasures of a freeman; my food was sweet, my labor pleasure: and one bright gleam of life seemed to shine upon me. However he not fulfilling his agreement, I let myself to Wm. Hooker, a Constable, with whom I worked only a few days--I directly contracted with Mr. Belias Hill, a shop joiner; but my stay with him was also of short duration; indeed it still seemed to me as it ever had done, that I was fortunes football, and must depend upon her gentle kicks. When I left Mr. Hill, I made an agreement with a Mr. Craw who was by trade a Tanner; determined to obtain some property, that I might in some measure enjoy the independence of the freedom I possessed. I purchased by agreement twenty five acres of land of Mr. Craw, which lay in the East Part of the town; for this land I was to work six months; he promising before witnesses to pay me $250, in failure of his procuring me a good indisputable title.

When I had paid for my land by faithfully laboring for the term agreed on: I made a tour to the pool at new Lebanon--from thence I returned to Dorset.--I bargained with John Manly a tavern-keeper, to work for him for some considerable time; in fact our agreement was that while each party was contented, I should serve him.

During my servile situation with Mr. Manly I became acquainted with Widow Susannah Dublin. In the spring I settled with Mr. Manly and returned to Poltney. On my arrival in Poultney Mr. Craw solicited me to work again for him, I preferring to work in a family with whom I had once been acquainted. I bargained and continued with him until fall--well may the reader imagine that during the suns diurnal course this summer I most fondly gazed on his last glittering beams at eve; and impatiently sighed to behold him peep from his eastern chambers, in the morn. Yes even at this late and advanced period of my life, the delightful idea of enjoying the bliss of hymen kindled warm and pleasing sensation in a heart that ever glowed in the participation of true and mutual friendship. So long had I been acquainted with, and so long had I been enerved to the keen smarts of disappointment: that it seemed impossible that I should ever realize the supreme joy of being united in the holy band of matrimony, to a native African female, who possessed a reciprocal abhorrence to slavery, and whose sufferings had been equal to any that can be delineated by the pen, or indured by the bravest of the human race, whose history I must omit as it will swell these memoirs beyond the bounds of my limits. But in justice to her memory, I think it my duty to observe that she proved to me, a virtuous patient, loving, and prudent wife, and industry was as habitual with her, as was tenderness and effection for her children. By her I was blessed with children, who prove a comfort to me in my declining years. To raise and educate my children, and instruct them in those moral virtues and religious principles, which should render them useful and honest citizens in this life, was my anxious care. And if possible to lay a foundation of religious virtue on which, with the blessings of a Saviour they might build a fabric which would insure them a blissful eternity. And it is my delight to say, I see none of them prone to the ways of evil doings.

I was married in the month of November, and moved my wife to Poltney soon after. I built me a snug log house, near one Mr. Solomon Norton, where I resided one year. At the expiration of which time, I was solicited to move into the middle of the town, which I did, and went to live with the Rev. Ithamer Hibbard, Pastor of the Presbyterian Church in that Town, with whom I resided about one year and six months. Nothing material transpired in that time. But at the close of this period, there came one of the most distressing famines, I ever knew, many people were in danger of starving, and others were obliged to live weeks without bread.

In the time of this famine among the people, I went to chopping Cole-wood, for Mr. Samuel Joslin, to get Iron to carry to Manchester, a distance of about 30 miles. When I got one hundred weight of Iron, it was my practice to take it upon my shoulder and carry it over the Mountains to Manchester, and get two bushels of Grain upon my back, and return to my family. Thus I supported them through this distressing time.

While in performing these duties, I became acquainted with my wife's old Mistress in Manchester, she owned part of a Grist-Mill, and requested me to move to Manchester, and remain untill a better opportunity offered me, to clear my Land. Accordingly I complied with her request, and we moved down soon after, by the assistance of one Mr. Daniel Beckwith. During my residence here, I raised good crops of Corn and other Grain, and life glided along greatly to my satisfaction.

And here it is a pleasure to observe, during all this time, after my good Mrs. Stiles died, who taught me to read and expound the Bible, I continued strictly to read the same and endeavor to learn its divinity.

While in this prosperous way, Mrs. Powell, entered a complaint to the Selectmen against me. She was instigated by a Mr. Dion, one of the selectmen.----The complaint amounted to this, that as I was a black man. The corruption and superstition, mingled with the old Connecticut bigotry and puritanism, made certain people think a Negro had no right to raise their own Children. Therefore I was complained of, that the selectmen might be enabled to bind out the children, which my wife had by her first husband. Dixon wanted the boy; that was the moving spring to the complaint.

As he was about twelve years of age, and began to be useful, and could earn more than his living, it was sufficient to induce almost any honest selectman to induce a complaint to be entered, that he might have the profits of his labors.

Dixon, and one Timothy Mead, came to my house one day to take him away, but I expostulated with them, and told them that it was unchristian in human religion, and unnatural for them to attempt it. As Moses had made his special cannon in which he was inspired by the father of the Universe, which was, that we must not afflict a fatherless child, or oppress a stranger. I quoted many passages of scripture, to prove the impropriety of a christian people holding in chains of bondage, their fellow beings, who are commanded to unite as one, and must partake of the blood of Christ our Saviour, and while thus partaking the Sacrament, hold the cup in one hand, and the scourge or whip, in the other; for cannot an African slave become a christian and member of the same church, with a miserable owner; certainly, and no man dare object to it. No! not even an Indian, Mahomitan, Turk or Ethiopian heathen would perform such a deed.--But all my intreaties were in vain. They scorned at my expostulation. They took away the boy and bound him out. One further reason I gave them, which was that I came to Manchester to stay for a season, and that I had Land in Poultney, which was paid for, and that I intended to move there immediately, and very much wanted the boys assistance in clearing the same. But Dixon told me it would be in vain for me to attempt to clear my land, as I had no Oxen, and without which, I could do nothing. I asked him how many young Americans, left their Father's dwellings, in the old towns, and travelled far into the Wilds of Vermont, and commenced clearing Farms for their future residence, with no other Tool of husbandry, save only the Ax upon his shoulder; and when he had walked over the lands of his anticipated residence, pitched upon some favorite spot for his, and his offspring's future dwellings, and when he struck his Ax into a fair towering Maple of the forest, whether his heart did not swell and vibrate with a glow of anticipated delight indiscribable. And if he would return me my poor little negro boy, my prospects would be as good as theirs. But I might as well laid pearl before Swine, as all this had no effect.

And to close the scene of oppression, my wife had a little girl by the name of Bersheba. She also, must be bound out by the authority, or by my consent, and to alleviate her situation, I consented to have her bound out to a Mrs. Powell, on her indenture or agreement to learn the girl to read, and to give her a good feather bed, when she should arrive at the age of eighteen, at which time she had fulfilled her indentures, and was free.

But that good Christian woman, never attempted to learn her to read, neither did she ever give her the bed. I could get no redress--for what Lawyer would undertake the cause of an old African Negro, against a respectable Widow in Manchester, who had many respectable acquaintances. None, for if there had been one, willing to take up in my defense, he would have been flung out of business, for taking up so dirty a cause against so respectable a personage as the Widow Powell, on no other evidence only the Negro's family, who might swear to the contract. Therefore as no gentleman of the Bar, would disgrace himself so much as to engage in the cause, Mrs. Powell went free, and escaped in her iniquity with impunity.

CONTENTS OF CHAPTER. 10.

CHAPTER. 10.

Soon after these Christian salutes, I returned to Poultney, settled upon my land and went to clearing it up as fast as was in my power. The first season I cleared about seven Acres, and sowed it with Wheat, enclosed the same with an excellent pole and log fence. But one Jery Goran, who wanted my land, & to whom I refused to sell it, pulled down my fence and let in cattle. The same year I had a crop of good Corn, which land I had cleared off early in the Spring, he also turned his cattle into that and destroyed it, so that I did not get five bushels from 8 Acres, which otherwise would have produced me more than one hundred bushels.

The next year Goram came to me, and wished to join with me in making Sugar, and offered to find Kettles, as I had none, also help me make troughs if I would find trees, and do a share of the work, which was agreed to, by me. At the close of the season, I had 8 lb. When we came to divide, as he and his family had found means to get away the remainder; as we had two hundred trees tapped, I thought the compliment was small, and expostulated but to no effect.

The next Spring, while I went to town to buy a Kettle, Susan went to tapping trees, as she said she had frequently made Sugar while with her old Master. Goram saw her at work, and came down to drive her off, as he said he had the possession there, and would not suffer her to work upon the land. She then asked him whether Jeffery had not bought that land of Mr. Craw. Goram said if he had, it was his land, and he would occupy it, and she should not tap the trees, and then attempted to take the pail, which contained the spouts from her. They both pulled and broke the bail; he got it away from her, and dashed it into the brook, which broke it into pieces. He also flung away her tapping Iron: at which she got away his Ax, and flung that into the brook after her things. Then he clinched, and attempted to fling her in after them all; but she proving two stout for him, like to have wrestled him into the brook; at any rate she got him down, and rubbed him well in the face and neck, with good white March Snow. She then threatened to complain to the authority; he tried to dissuade her but to no effect, as she was determined to have redress, and went to Capt. Josiah Grant, and entered a complaint.

It was late when I returned; or before I slept I should have avenged the injury. The majesty of Guina rose indignant in my breast, and I was determined to give him a drubbing. But the next morning, Capt. Grant and Joseph Adams, came up and we left the matter to them, as neighbors; who said we ought under all circumstances, keep peace in the neighborhood. As Goram claimed a share in the Troughs, he must ask Susan's pardon, and occupy one share of the sugar place for that season. Thus this affair was settled.

After spring opened, I went to the Town of Wells, which was situated south of Poultney, on the line of the state of New York, where I purchased me a very handsome yoke of young oxen. After I had been in possession of my oxen a few days, I purchased me twenty five Apple Trees, and while setting them out, I directed my Boys to drive the oxen down into my meadow, in order to bate them before I went to plowing. While thus baiting, the division fence between Goram and myself, not being made, as it belonged to him to make that part--my cattle got across the line into his meadow; he ran after them flung a large stone, and broke the leg of one of them, which matter we left to men, Judge Ward and Stephen Clark, who decided that he must give me fifteen dollars and take the Ox. Mortified at this decision, Goram entered a complaint to the selectmen, in order to get my children bound out by the town. The authority came to me about the business; but I plainly told them, that as I had suffered so much by bondage myself, my children should never be under the direction of any other person whilst I lived. That if they would keep Goram from destroy my property, I could support my family, as well as Goram could his, and they never wanted for wholesome food, as clean linen, neither were they backward in education.

Some short time after, my Pigs got out of the pasture, and went into Goram's corn; as soon as it was discovered by my family, my wife went after them. Mrs. Goram had caught one; Susan expostulated with her, but she would not let her have the pig; therefore, Susan took the Pig by the hind legs, and forced it from her. For this affair, Goram and his wife brought an action of assault and battery, against me and my wife, for the assault and battery committed by

124

Susan, wife of Jeffery Brace, upon the body of Goram's wife. But on the trial it appearing that there was no assault; the court acquitted us, and immersed him with costs, which judgment so vexed Goram, that he again complained to the authority, in order to get my children bound out; the selectmen came, and when we were arguing upon the subject, I asked, if they were strangers in Africa, whether they would be willing to have their children bound out to Negroes; they said that was a different case, for white men were more capable than Africans, of taking care themselves. I turned with indignation from them and their arguments, by telling them that while I lived, no authority should bind out my children. After this Goram went to Middletown, and got one Clark to come to Poultney to try me, which he did, and Judged me to pay twelve dollars; thus I was hunted down at last.

The next spring, I said to one of my neighbors, if Goram pulled down my fence and destroyed my crops that year. I should be tempted to burn his barn. For this I was arrested, and tried by two justices, who, on a fair and full examination of the matter, honorably acquitted me,

At length Goram swore, he would whip me, and when I went up to him, in order to take it, he would run away from me, and thereby save me from a good drubbing; and to wind up this scene of difficulty, we had each of us, an excellent ram, they met, and as I suppose mine so maimed his that he died of the wounds. It was secretly reported around the neighborhood, that Old Jef. had killed Goram's Ram, and his wife had made the meat into Mints pies for Thanksgiving; and one David Varnum, was sent as a spy, in order to enquire of my wife, where she got the meet to make her mints Pies, she very ingeniously told him, that Jeffery had wrought for Major Dewey, who paid him in Beef, which proving to be the truth, put an end to their slander.

As it was against the Law in Vermont, to let Rams go at large in a certain season of the year; mine was fastened to a stake in my Meadow near the house. One night the stake was pulled up and the Ram went off. While my boys were looking for him in the morning; Goram gave them the halter, with which he was held, but said he had not seen the Ram; in consequence of which my Ram got among his sheep and was forfeited.

These insults were more patiently borne by me, than they were by my children, whose feelings were alive to every opprobrium that was cast upon their Father; they would often threaten to avenge my wrongs, but this I always discouraged. Frequently would I expostulate with them, and instruct them the lessons of divine patience. I told them the best way for us, as we were of a sable race, to get redress was, to return good for evil, and thereby shame and mortify the ostentatious destroyer of our rights. This to them seemed like false doctrine. However they generally paid due attention to my instruction.

But to end this disagreeable relation, I, after living about seven years in this unhappy situation, by the side of Goram, who was determined to be a thorn in my side.

I sold my land to the best advantage possible, and was determined to move to some distant part of the country where I might enjoy the evening of life, in a more tranquil and peaceable manner, than I possible could do in this place. I got about half of the value of my land; as Goram pretended to have an adverse claim;--therefore no man would give me the value of it, and have to quiet Goram.

When I had sold, I talked some of going to Kentucky with Colonel Mathew Lyon. But I did not know that being so near slavery again, they might haul me in; or that I should say something which would cause me to be prosecuted and punished as a seditious person. Therefore, after all matters were settled in Poultney, I removed to Sheldon in Vermont, a new town, about 114 miles north of Poultney. As I never received half of the value of my land, and after arriving with my family in Sheldon, a new town, almost destitute of provisions, I underwent many difficulties for the want of the remainder: being among strangers who felt but little kindness for people of my color. However fortune placed me in a happy spot.

I went to live on some land belonging to Major Jedediah Clark, who had been a neighbor to me. I also lived near Josiah Tuttle, Esq. who was to me a benefactor. As I was greatly indebted to him for many acts of kindness.

On this land I resided almost two years, when I purchased fifty acres of Land of Major Samuel Shelden. I paid him down in cash twenty five dollars, and he was to wait six years for the remainder, the price being five dollars per Acre, I cleared about ten acres fit for corn; but there came a Man, and wanted the whole lot; his name was Crocker, and Shelden sold him the whole lot, and told me, he would pay me for the betterments, and let me have a lot near the middle of the town, which was never performed:

yet I have that charity for the memory of Major Shelden, that if he had lived, he would have amply satisfied me.

Finding I could not get the land contemplated I removed in the Spring of 1804, to Georgia, a pleasant situated town on the Banks of Lake Champlain, where I purchased with my son-in-law, sixty acres of land of Esq. Evtets, and where I contemplated spending my days.

Here I settled down in the peaceful sunshine of anticipated delight. Industry caused prosperity to hover round my cot. But alas! when gliding along in the peace and sunshine of earthly felicity-- veiled were the Heavens in black. The partner of my life was called from me, and her soul wafted into a boundless eternity. Short was the warning, but heavy the blow. She was taken sick on the 8th of March, 1807, and died 19th of the same month. The throbbing and tender emotion of my bosom during her illness, are indescribable, but death sealed the fate as indelible; and it was my duty to be content, but I was left without an earthly companion, to linger out the remainder of my days.

CONTENTS OF CHAPTER. 11.

CHAPTER. 11.

Here I think it my duty to take a review of my life, so far as to give an account of my religious experiences. As before observed, during my residence with the Widow Stiles, she taught me to read the Bible, as that contained those religious truths, which were necessary for the salvation of my soul. She also had me baptized according to the religious tenants of the church to which she belonged. During my services in the American war, I paid but little attention to her instructions. But after my emancipation and arrival at Poultney and during my residence with the good old Mr. Joseph Craw, I not speaking very good English, for my own Amusement and instruction, employed all my leisure hours, in reading the Bible. This opened my eyes in some degree, and I began seriously to reflect on my situation, as it related to man, and what I was to my Creator. The first aid I received from scripture, was Moses' declaration "the Lord our God, has no respect of persons." Then I read in the tenth chapter of the Acts of the apostles, the following truth:

Ver 34. Then Peter opened his mouth, and said, Of a truth I perceive that God is no respecter of persons:

35 But in every nation he that feareth him, and worketh righteousness, is accepted with him.

36 The word which God sent unto the children of Israel, preaching peace by Jesus Christ; (he is Lord of all;)

37 That word, I say, ye know, which was published throughout all Judea, and began from Galilee, after the baptism which John preached;

38 How God anointed Jesus of Nazareth with the Holy Ghost, and with power; who went about doing good, and healing all that were oppressed of the devil: for God was with him.

39 And we are witnesses of all things which he did, both in the land of the Jews and in Jerusalem; whom they slew, and hanged on a tree:

40 Him God raised up the third day, and shewed him openly;

41 Not to all the people, but unto witnesses chosen before of God, even to us who did eat and drink with him after he rose from the dead.

42 And he commanded us to peach unto the people, and to testify that it is he which was ordained of God to be the Judge of quick and dead.

43 To him give all the prophets witness, that through his name, whose ever believeth in him shall receive remission of sins.

44 While Peter yet spake these words, the Holy Ghost fell on all them which heard the word.

45 And they of the circumcision which believed were astonished, as many as came with Peter, because that on the Gentiles also was poured out the gifts of Holy ghost.

45 For they heard them speak with tongues, and magnify God. Then answered Peter,

47 Can any man forbid water, that these should not be baptized, which have received the Holy Ghost as well as we?

48 And he commanded them to be baptized in the name of the Lord. Then prayed they him to tarry certain days.

When I seriously reflected upon the assurances contained in the foregoing scripture, my eyes were opened, and I was encouraged and verily believed, that I was equally acceptable with all mankind.

Revelations, Chap. 4, Ver. 2.

Thou art worthy, O Lord, to receive glory, and honor, and power; for thou hast created all things; and for thy pleasure they are and were created. Also, I read, that God made man after his own image, and breathed the breath of life into him, and man became a living soul. Here I reflected there was nothing intimated what color either God or man was. And in Psalms, it is said--"Look unto me all ye ends of the earth, and believe and ye shall be saved, for I am God, and none else besides me."

Thus I was strengthened, I reflected upon my lonesome situation among the sons of men, I could discover no hope of consolation only in a redeemer, I ventured to address the throne of grace. I began to behold the beauty, power, majesty, and glory of an all wise and just God, who is able to save me, even in the remotest ends of the earth; who had supported and protected me through all trials and suffering while in the hands of my tyrants, groaning under the lash of unnatural masters, I fancied my life had been preserved by his Almighty shield for some good ends, I hoped I was to be made an instrument for the redemption of my African brethren, from the gauling chains of bondage; or for conveying the light of Christianity to my native land. This taste of divine goodness gave me courage. "Ask and ye shall receive, seek and ye shall find, knock and it shall be opened unto you."

St. John, 3d Chap. 16th verse.

For God so loved the world, that he gave his only begatten son, that whosoever believeth in him should not perish, but have everlasting life.

17th For God sent not his son into the world to condemn the world, but that the world through him might be saved.

Here I thought it my duty to pray to God, in and through the Savior Jesus Christ: Accordingly I went down into a distant meadow, chose a silent spot, by the side of a large birch log; the sun was just setting, and the heavens seemed to be perfectly serene, all nature were retiring to rest. I kneeled me down and attempted in humble adoration to offer up my fervent ejulations, to the throne of grace. I prayed for all mankind, for all my African brethren, whether at home, or in foreign lands, groaning out a miserable existence in slavery; in short for all heathen and Christian nations, that those in darkness might receive the knowledge of the Mediator and savior Jesus Christ.

This was on Friday evening, I felt some relief, but I was in great darkness, and heavily pressed with the weight of my sins.

On Saturday morning Mr. Craw told me, he wanted me to go to the north of his farm and get some lime stones, we went and wrought all day. On Saturday evening I met some of my associates, who invited me to go and amuse ourselves on the sabbath as we were wont to do. I felt such a weight of guilt pressing upon me, I could not admonish them, I therefore turned from them, and gave an evasive or no answer.

On Sunday morning, Mr. Craw, that good old Christian, addressed the throne of grace. I secretly prayed in my heart that my load of guilt might be removed, that I could join with him in Christian faith. But such was my situation, all my iniquities stared me full in the face. I sunk before it and acknowledged my guilt. On Monday morning, I went into the woods to cut some timber, to use about the lime pit. The wind blew upon the tops of the trees, and I thought they cursed me; in short it seemed as though all nature held me in abhorrence. I dare not begin to chop, and walked backwards and forwards for some time. I dare not attempt to pray, it appeared my prayers would be the height of iniquity; I thought Mr. Craw would blame me if I did not work. At length I ventured to say the Lord's prayer, this gave me considerable relief. I then began to chop, Mr. Craw's son came down, and we wrought until noon; we went up to dinner, but I could not eat one morsel. Mrs. Craw took notice of it, and enquired the cause, I could not say one word. In the afternoon, I took the oxen and went to drawing the timber we had chopped. All nature seemed to frown upon me, I was so weak I could not load the logs upon the sled. Young Craw come to my assistance, we continued our labor, until night, I went to the barn to turn out the cattle and fodder. After I had flung down the hay and while still on the Mow, I ventured to pray, I prayed for some time. All at once, I felt light as air, I prayed more fervently, a region of happiness seemed to be opened before me. My load of guilt was removed, and I thought I heard a voice say, God can be just and justify the chief of sinners. That night I enjoyed all the sweets, and felt, all the consolation which appertains to man this side of the Grave. I prayed and felt the immediate assistance of the redeeming spirit of all perfection, I was strengthened by faith, and hope seemed to soothe all my anxieties. I remained in this situation for some weeks; my knowledge of Christ seemed to increase daily.

Then I began to think of Baptism, as before observed, I had once been Baptized, but for what reason I then did not understand; I viewed it as a favor of my good mistress Stiles. And if I had been told that it was a covenant necessary to be performed, I did not understand it; therefore I thought at this time, it was my duty to search for myself; I read in Mathew:--Go ye therefore, and teach all nations, and he that believeth, and is baptized shall be saved. I also read in the four Evangelists, the same doctrine.

Then I began to reflect what belief was, and what we must believe; and it seemed to me that I must believe in the Lord Jesus Christ as the son of God, as the only Mediator and Savior of mankind. Then what is baptism. I read in the 3d Chap. Mathew, the following Scripture--Ver. 13 Then cometh Jesus from Galilee to Jorden unto John, to be baptized of him:

14 But John forbade him saying, I have need to be baptized of thee, and comest thou to me.

15. And Jesus answering, said unto him, suffer it to be so now: for thus it becommeth us to fulfill all righteousness. Then he suffered him.

16 And Jesus, when he was baptized, went up strait way out of the water: and Lo! the Heavens were opened unto him, and he saw the spirit of God descending like a dove, and lighting upon him.

17 And Lo! a voice from Heaven, saying, this is my beloved Son, in whom I am well pleased.

Believing it my duty as much as possible to follow the examples of the savior, I was convinced by the foregoing scripture that plunging or being immersed in water, was the true baptism contemplated in the gospel, therefore I concluded to follow the example (in this respect) of the redeemer. Also the Apostle Paul said, "Be ye buried with Christ in baptism.

I continued in this belief searching for a church with whom I could commune, until my settling in Georgia before mentioned, there I believed it my duty to enter into full communion. Accordingly on the 6th of June 1805, I was baptized in Georgia, by the Rev. Elder David Hulebert, Pastor of the Baptist Church in Swanton, by which I became a member of the Baptist Church in Georgia with which I have walked to this time endeavoring as much as possible, not to fall out by the way.

And now after having passed through so many varying scenes of life, and having lost my beloved companion, as before mentioned, and being left as it were, alone in this world. I have concluded it my duty to myself, to all Africans, who can read, to the Church, in short to all mankind, to thus publish these my Memoirs, that all may see how poor Africans have been, and perhaps now are abused by a Christian and enlightened people. Being old and blind, almost destitute of property, it may bring me something to make me comfortable in my declining days, but above all, it is my anxious wish, that this simple narrative, may be the means of opening the hearts of those who hold slaves and move them to consent to give them that freedom which they themselves enjoy, and which all mankind have an equal right to possess.

Jeremiah, 9th Chap. Ver. 1st. Oh that my head were waters, and mine eyes a fountain of tears, that I might weep day and night for the slain of the daughter of my people.

MIRIFICA SUNT OPERA DEI.

APOLOGY.

THE writer of the foregoing memoirs, deems it his duty to Apologize to those who read them, for many apparent repetition in the narrative which were unavoidable, as the narrator not speaking plain English, it was extremely difficult to get a regular chain of his ideas; also in relating, he would frequently recollect circumstances, which he had omitted in their proper places.

But the writer has taken unwearied pains to render it as amusing and correct as possible; Carefully avoiding every circumstance which might tend to wound the feelings of any individual or society of men.

The scripture is inserted by the request of the narrator, and under his immediate direction and every fact recorded according to his relation, and much in his own language.

The Author.

www.ingramcontent.com/pod-product-compliance
Lightning Source LLC
Chambersburg PA
CBHW031210270326
41931CB00006B/506

www.ingramcontent.com/pod-product-compliance
Lightning Source LLC
Chambersburg PA
CBHW062057270326
41931CB00013B/3115